What Others Are Saying

"Dr. Eddie Estep has given us a useful, well-written, and insightful review of the influencers in the life of David, Israel's king. This is a very good book with a fresh approach. I highly recommend it!"

—Jesse C. Middendorf
Director, Center for Pastoral Leadership, Nazarene Theological Seminary
General Superintendent Emeritus, Church of the Nazarene

"Dr. Estep's great insight into leadership is that leading is fundamentally about relationships. . . . *Who's Got Your Back?* uses the iconic figure of David to demonstrate that relationships are at the very core of David's great successes—and his tragic failures. Whether you lead a church board or a combat formation, David's leadership bears careful consideration."

—Joe McLamb
Combat veteran

"These powerful 100 leadership principles will prove a blessing to the church as they are discovered by preachers, staff teams, students, lay leaders, and even devotional readers."

—Bob Broadbooks
Regional Director, USA/Canada Region, Church of the Nazarene
Author, *How to Bless Your Pastor*

"Eddie Estep has crafted the story of one of my favorite biblical leaders and those who impacted him into an exciting, easy-to-read action adventure guide to great leadership."

—Larry Rinehart
Chief of Police, Bexley, Ohio
Author, *The Power of Vision in Leadership*

"Estep offers unique insights into those who influenced this 'man after God's own heart.' These lessons could be used for staff meetings, small groups, men's discipleship, or for personal growth. It is my privilege to recommend this book to everyone who loves the Word of God and seeks to develop authentic, biblical leadership skills."

—David Graves
General Superintendent, Church of the Nazarene

"*Who's Got Your Back?* is a valuable resource for leaders confronted with the challenge of reaching their fullest potential and should be on the shelf of every pastor desiring to meet the important challenge of discipling and raising up leaders."

—Don Richter
President and Director, Harvest Preparation International Ministries

"Dr. Estep articulates multiple lessons from biblical times that will help the reader to easily apply attributes and important core leadership values to today's culture."

—F. Michael Doran
Regional President, Metropolitan Edison Company

"'You can't make this stuff up.' That's what people in the local church say about the odd challenges they experience along the way as an awkward conglomeration of saints marches into the kingdom of God. I suppose that's why we love David. He faced it all. . . . And in the heart of our story, he is described as the man after God's own heart. . . . Eddie Estep has given us a concentrated look."

—Dan Boone
President, Trevecca Nazarene University
Author, *A Charitable Discourse*

"Through biblical narrative, Eddie Estep inspires leaders to lead in the context that 'life is relationships.'. . . The well-chosen and numerous applications will make an ongoing marked difference to the effectiveness of a leader."

—Nina G. Gunter
General Superintendent Emerita, Church of the Nazarene

WHO'S GOT YOUR BACK?
LEADERSHIP LESSONS FROM THE LIFE OF KING DAVID

EDDIE ESTEP

BEACON HILL PRESS
OF KANSAS CITY

Beacon Hill Press of Kansas City
PO Box 419527
Kansas City, MO 64141
www.BeaconHillBooks.com

ISBN 978-0-8341-3361-7

Printed in the
United States of America

Cover Design: Ryan Deo
Interior Design: Sharon Page

Unless otherwise indicated all Scripture quotations are from *The Holy Bible, New International
Version®* (NIV®). Copyright © 1973, 1978, 1984, 2011 by Biblica, Inc.™ Used by permission.
All rights reserved worldwide.

Permission to quote from the following additional copyrighted versions of the Bible is
acknowledged with appreciation:

The *New American Standard Bible®* (NASB®). Copyright © The Lockman Foundation 1960,
1962, 1963, 1968, 1971, 1972, 1973, 1975, 1977, 1995.

The *New King James Version* (NKJV). Copyright © 1979, 1980, 1982 Thomas Nelson, Inc.

The Message (TM). Copyright © 1993, 1994, 1995, 1996, 2000, 2001, 2002. Used by permission of NavPress Publishing Group.

Library of Congress Cataloging-in-Publication Data

Estep, Eddie.
    Who's got your back? : leadership lessons from the life of King David / Eddie Estep.
       pages cm
    Includes bibliographical references.
    ISBN 978-0-8341-3361-7 (pbk.)
    1. David, King of Israel—Friends and associates. 2. Leadership—Biblical teaching. I. Title.
    BS580.D3E795 2014
    248.4—dc23
                                                                    2014021905

The Internet addresses, email addresses, and phone numbers in this book are
accurate at the time of publication. They are provided as a resource. Beacon
Hill Press of Kansas City does not endorse them or vouch for their content or
permanence.

10 9 8 7 6 5 4 3 2 1

The book is lovingly dedicated to

Diane, whose love, partnership, and companionship is
a means of grace. God has used your wisdom, understanding,
and example to shape me into a better leader.

And to Josh and Jeff, who continue to teach me lessons about
leadership, authenticity, and self-awareness that are best learned
from loving sons. Your leadership potential is huge. No father
could ask for two finer sons, or love them more.

Has there ever been another man blessed with such great travel
companions on the journey of life?

*"The boundary lines have fallen for me in pleasant places;
surely I have a delightful inheritance."*
—David (Ps. 16:6)

CONTENTS

ACKNOWLEDGMENTS

My deep appreciation goes to Nazarene congregations that gave me an opportunity to serve and to learn, through trial and error, many of the lessons contained in this book: Ripley, West Virginia; Maysville, Kentucky; and Columbus, Ohio (Shepherd).

I want to thank my wife, Diane, a woman of great relational intelligence, for her constant encouragement. She was the first reader of each chapter and offered many helpful comments.

I am especially indebted to Peggy Smith—who has a contagious love for the South in general and South Carolina in particular—for proofing and editing early drafts of the manuscript.

I want to thank my dad and mom, Donald and Joyce Estep, whose examples in the home, the church, and the workplace provided my earliest models for leadership.

My gratitude is expressed to Geoff Kunselman, Joe McLamb, Don Richter, Steve Estep, Scott Estep, and Kim Duey, who read drafts of the manuscript and offered valuable comments and suggestions.

I would be remiss if I did not mention those whose leadership has greatly influenced me: Leroy Hostutler, LeBron Fairbanks, Jim Couchenour, Greg Rosser, Paul Cunningham, Tom Nees, Dan Boone, Jesse Middendorf, Gustavo Crocker, Ken Mills, Bob Broadbooks, Christian Sarmiento, Nina Gunter, and Joe McLamb, to name just a few.

Finally, to the South Carolina District Church of the Nazarene—especially its pastors—thank you for the privilege of serving you and exercising the leadership lessons in this book.

INTRODUCTION

King David has been an intriguing personality and the focus of attention for authors, artists, preachers, and readers. No other person, with the exception of Jesus, garners more biblical attention than David. Sixty-two chapters of the Old Testament are devoted to telling the story of his life, and at least fifty-four references in the New Testament call attention to him.

One of the enduring qualities of David's story is that he is observable in so many seasons of life. He was a shepherd, a giant slayer, a poet, a warrior, an adulterer, a musician, and a king. Even with all of his strengths and successes, all of his flaws and failures, and all their tragic consequences, Israel adored him like no other king she ever had.

While many have endeavored to tell the story of David according to the events of his life, this book will endeavor to tell the story of David according to the relationships of his life. Leadership does not occur in a vacuum; it takes place in the arena of relationships. The leader is shaped, and shapes, through relationships. Nowhere in the Bible is this more apparent than in the example of David, king of Israel.

This book examines the dynamics of David's relationships with friends, family, foes, associates, and acquaintances, then explores the leadership lessons from those relationships. Each chapter will highlight a person who appears in the Old Testament account of David, examine the nature of that person's relationship with David, explore the leadership lessons discovered in that relationship, suggest questions for leadership development, and conclude with a psalm related to that chapter. Rather than provide a myriad of illustrations from my personal experience, I have largely chosen to let David's story speak for itself. Readers will undoubtedly be able to supply ample illustrations from their own experience for each of the leadership lessons.

Leaders must be concerned about everything from vision to strategy to morale to team building to motivation to management to methods to mission to delegation, as well as the leader's own ability to learn and develop and grow. Like most leaders, David provides some excellent examples of all of these; but, also like most leaders, sometimes he fails spectacularly. We can learn from both, striving to emulate the former while avoiding the latter.

It is my hope that pastors will find this book to be beneficial for personal devotions, church board development, and as a resource for sermon development. Leaders of small groups and Sunday school classes will find within these pages a curriculum for the study of David's life. Ministry teams, pastoral staffs, and organizational groups will find this to be a resource for leadership development using biblically based principles.

It was said of David that he shepherded the people "with integrity of heart; with skillful hands he led them" (Ps. 78:72). The world needs more leaders with strength of character (integrity of heart) and compelling competence (skillful hands). If this book somehow contributes to the raising up of men and women who lead with both character and competence, the hope of this author will have been realized.

Eddie Estep
West Columbia, South Carolina

CAST OF CHARACTERS

Abiathar—son of Ahimelek, sole survivor of the massacre at Nob, served as high priest during David's reign

Abigail—widow of Nabal, became David's third wife

Abinadab—David's brother, Jesse's second son

Abinadab—son of Saul

Abishag—beautiful young virgin who served as David's nurse

Abishai—David's nephew, brother of Joab and Asahel, one of David's most trusted warriors

Abner—commander of Saul's army, Saul's cousin, murdered by Joab

Absalom—son of David, led a rebellion against David

Achish—Philistine ruler of Gath, provided sanctuary for David

Adonijah—son of David, challenged his brother Solomon for the throne

Adriel—husband of Merab, King Saul's son-in-law

Ahimelek—priest of Nob who supplied David with bread and sword, murdered by Doeg

Ahinoam—Saul's wife

Ahinoam of Jezreel—David's second wife

Ahithophel—one of David's chief advisers, joined Absalom's conspiracy, grandfather of Bathsheba

Amasa—army commander for Absalom and David, murdered by Joab

Amnon—son of David, raped Tamar, murdered by Absalom

Asahel—brother of Joab and Abishai, killed in battle by Abner

Baanah—with his brother, Rekab, assassinated Ish-Bosheth

Bathsheba—widow of Uriah, wife of David, mother of Solomon

Benaiah—one of David's elite warriors, Solomon's "Enforcer"

Boaz—father of Obed, grandfather of Jesse, great-grandfather of David

Doeg—Saul's henchman, murdered the priests and inhabitants of Nob

Eli—spiritual leader of Israel, priest who raised Samuel

Eliab—brother of David, eldest son of Jesse

Eliam—one of David's "Thirty" elite warriors, father of Bathsheba

Elkanah—father of Samuel, husband of Hannah

Gad—prophet who confronts David in the matter of the census

Goliath—Philistine giant killed by David

Haggith—wife of David, mother of Adonijah

Hannah—mother of Samuel, wife of Elkanah

Hushai—friend and counselor of David, sent by David to spy on Absalom and frustrate the advice of Ahithophel

Ish-Bosheth—son of Saul, succeeded him as king of Israel

Ishbi-Benob—Philistine giant who threatened David, killed by Abishai

Ittai—Gittite, commander in David's army

Jedidiah—God's name for Solomon

Jesse—father of David

Joab—David's nephew, commanding general of David's army, brother of Abishai and Asahel, murdered Abner and Amasa

Jonadab—brought news of Amnon's death to David

Jonathan—son of Saul, friend of David

Kish—Saul's father

Maakah—wife of David, mother of Absalom

Malki-Shua—son of Saul

Mephibosheth—crippled son of Jonathan

Merab—oldest daughter of Saul

Michal—David's first wife, daughter of Saul

Nabal—wealthy husband of Abigail, disrespected David

Nahash—Ammonite king who threatened Jabesh Gilead

Nathan—prophet who confronts David over his sin with Bathsheba

Obed—son of Boaz, father of Jesse, grandfather of David

Paltiel—given Michal (David's first wife) in marriage by Saul

Rekab—with his brother, Baanah, assassinated Ish-Bosheth

Rehoboam—son of Solomon, succeeds Solomon as king of Israel

Rimmon—a Benjamite, father of Baanah and Rekab

Rizpah—Saul's concubine

Samuel—last of the judges, first of the prophets, anointed both Saul and David as king

Saul—first king of Israel

Shammah—David's brother, Jesse's third son

Sheba—led a revolt against David

Shimei—cursed David as he was fleeing Jerusalem during Absalom's rebellion

Solomon—son of David and Bathsheba, succeeded David as king of Israel

Talmai—king of Geshur, maternal grandfather of Absalom

Tamar—daughter of David, raped by her half-brother, Amnon

Uriah—husband of Bathsheba, death arranged by David, one of David's "Thirty" elite warriors

Zadok—served with Abiathar as high priest during David's reign, served alone during Solomon's reign

Zeruiah—sister of David, mother of Abishai, Joab, and Asahel

Ziba—household servant of Saul, steward of Mephibosheth's property

— ONE —

SAMUEL

GOD KNOWS WHERE TO FIND YOU

The Background

The story of Samuel is told in 1 Samuel. He is also mentioned in 1 Chronicles 6:27, 28, 33; 7:2; 9:22; 11:3; 26:28; 29:29; 2 Chronicles 35:18; Psalm 99:6; Jeremiah 15:1; Acts 3:24; 13:20; and Hebrews 11:32.

The Story

Samuel was Israel's last judge, Israel's first prophet, and a member of Israel's long line of priests—a veritable one-man spiritual band.[1] Yahweh's representative and the de facto leader of Israel, he served a very important transitional role in Israel's history. By the time he anointed David king of Israel, Samuel was already long retired. He thought his service to Israel had concluded years before, but that was not to be. Again and again after his farewell address to the nation, Samuel was called back to duty for God and for his community.

From his earliest memories, Samuel had an awareness that God was going to use him in a special way. He had been told of how his mother, Hannah, had prayed for a son each year as she and his father, Elkanah, made their annual pilgrimage to worship at Shiloh. She prayed with such fervor that Eli the priest thought her a common drunk. In the course of time, God answered her prayer, and Hannah gave birth to Samuel. As she had promised, while he was still very young, she brought Samuel to Shiloh to be dedicated and raised by Eli.

Early in his life Samuel was recognized as a prophet to whom, and through whom, God spoke. As a young boy, Samuel first heard the call of God one night as he slept in the house of the Lord. The Lord had a message for Eli that Samuel faithfully delivered, at Eli's urging.

Later, upon the death of Eli and his two corrupt sons, Samuel gained national prominence as the spiritual leader of the nation. He called the nation to repentance and guided Israel to a great victory over the Philistines at Mizpah, bringing about the return of the ark of the covenant. He erected a large stone at the battle site as a memorial, and there ensued a long period of peace with Samuel annually traveling Israel as circuit judge.

As Samuel neared retirement, the people began clamoring for a king. There were a couple of reasons for this. First, Samuel's two greedy sons were not much better than Eli's sons in their dishonesty and propensity to pervert justice. They were in line to succeed Samuel as judge, and Israel wanted no part of either of them. Instead, looking at the surrounding nations, and seeing that monarchies were all the political rage, Israel decided that they wanted a king just like everybody else. Samuel accused Israel of wanting to look to a human king rather than to God, expressing his contempt for the idea of monarchy and warning the people of what having a king would cost them. Nevertheless, they insisted on a king and God gave them what they wanted. God directed Samuel to Saul, an impressive young man of the tribe of Benjamin, handsome and a head taller than any other Israelite.

Soon after Samuel anointed Saul king at Mizpah, Samuel gave his farewell speech, reminding Israel of their heritage and exhorting them to be faithful to God. The pouring of the horn of olive oil over Saul's head was Samuel's last act before retiring from public service. But it would not be long before Samuel would again be called to serve.

The first time Samuel was called back to duty was to address the Philistine threat at Gilgal. Saul's behavior at Gilgal only confirmed Samuel's earlier misgivings. Rather than obeying Samuel's instructions and waiting for the priest to arrive to make the sacrifices, Saul grew impatient and made the sacrifices himself. When Samuel arrived, he rebuked Saul for his disobedience and impatience.

The second time Samuel was called back to duty was to address the sin of Saul regarding the Amalekites. When Saul blatantly disregarded the instructions to completely annihilate the Amalekites and totally destroy their possessions, Samuel confronted the king and announced that his sin had disqualified him for the kingship.

The third and final time Samuel was called back to duty was to consecrate the successor of Saul. When Saul was rejected by God because of his disobedience, Samuel wiped away his last tears of disappointment over Israel's first king, refilled his horn with oil, and set out for Bethlehem, having been instructed by God that the new king would be one of Jesse's sons. Because he was afraid that King Saul might kill him if he suspected the true reason for his arrival in Bethlehem, the stated purpose for his visit to Bethlehem was to offer a sacrifice. Samuel took a young cow with him for the sacrifice and invited Jesse and his sons to the ceremony. Seven of Jesse's sons were present and passed before Samuel, but none of them were chosen. Samuel asked if there were any other sons, and Jesse told of David, the youngest, who was watching the sheep. Samuel knew immediately that he had found God's choice for king. Samuel's horn of oil was put to use a second time, and David, in the presence of his father and brothers, was anointed king.

As he stood looking at young David, Samuel must have been overwhelmed with the realization that this young man—young enough to be Samuel's grandson—was the future promise of Israel. What a contrast between David and Saul. David was a generation younger than Saul, a head shorter, full of innocence, unassuming and pure. From that day on the Spirit of the Lord came upon David with power, and Samuel returned home to live out his days in Ramah.

Sometime later, however, David forced Samuel out of retirement by fleeing to him at Ramah when Saul was trying to kill David; Samuel agreed to help him and, together, the two of them went to Naioth. Saul sent men to Naioth to capture Samuel and David, but instead Saul's men began to prophesy with Samuel and the prophets. Saul was exasperated, especially after it happened a second and a third time. Finally, Saul himself went to Naioth, and the same thing happened to him. Instead of capturing David and Samuel, Saul stripped off his own clothes and, in the presence of Samuel, began to prophesy.

At Samuel's death, all Israel gathered to mourn him and bury him at Ramah; but even now, Samuel would be called, once more, back into service. Saul, fearful of the outcome of a looming battle with the Philistines, asked a medium in Endor to conjure up Samuel in a séance. While alive, Samuel seldom had good news for Saul; that pattern only continued when Samuel was summoned from the dead. Samuel told Saul that he and his sons would meet their end at the hands of the Philistines and that the kingdom would pass into the hands of David. In life, not one of Samuel's words had "fall[en] to the ground" (1 Sam. 3:19). The same would prove true in death.

Leadership Lessons

1. God knows where to find you.

God found Samuel, though Samuel was just a boy sleeping near the ark of the covenant in the house of the Lord. God found Moses, though Moses was at the far side of the desert watching his father-in-law's herds. God found David, though David was in the fields watching his father's flocks. These were all found by God and called by God to significant leadership. None of them sought the responsibility God gave them, but each was willing to accept the responsibility, once called.

Would-be leaders sometimes attempt to "position" themselves for opportunity, making great efforts to be at the right place at the right time. The opposite was true for Moses, Samuel, and David, all of whom were sought out by God for significant places of leadership. As we will see later, even after David had been anointed king, he was willing to wait patiently for God to open doors before he assumed the throne.

Great leaders seldom seek great responsibility. Instead, great responsibility seeks them. Great leaders are often too busy faithfully accomplishing their present mission to seek assignments of greater responsibility. Ulysses S. Grant observed, "It is men who wait to be selected, and not those who seek, from whom we may always expect the most efficient service."[2]

There seem to be two paths to leadership. One path is traveled by those who hasten to bring about leadership opportunities. These individuals seek authority for the perceived benefits associated with those positions. The other path is traveled by those who trust providence and the will of God to bring to pass the leadership opportunities. As I heard a friend say, "God always saves the best for those who give the choice to him."[3]

A. W. Tozer wrote,

> A true and safe leader is likely to be one who has no desire to lead but is forced into a position of leadership by the inward pressure of the Spirit and the press of the external situation. Such were Moses and David and the Old Testament prophets. I believe it might be accepted as a fairly reliable rule of thumb that the man who is ambitious to lead is disqualified as a leader.[4]

2. Emerging leaders need experienced leaders to bless them.

Being anointed with oil by the spiritual leader of the nation would have been a visible sign of blessing and a significant call to leadership. Samuel might have said to David "God has called you to this, and given you this special opportunity to serve him. He is with you. Be strong. Take courage." For young David to be blessed by the aged prophet Samuel would have provided the confirmation of his call that young David would carry in his heart and his memory until he himself reached old age.

David and Samuel may never have seen each other prior to the day of David's anointing in Bethlehem. But that day was the beginning of a very special relationship. It was to Samuel that David, while running for his life from Saul, first turned for refuge. The blessing of an experienced leader is a significant gift to an emerging leader. Such a blessing can provide encouragement and confidence for the challenges that lie ahead.

3. The leaders of the next generation might not resemble the leaders of this generation.

When Samuel began to size up Jesse's sons, he was first drawn to the tall, handsome, elder brother, Eliab, who stood head and shoulders taller than the others. Eliab appeared to be the best choice for king and even resembled King Saul. David's leadership potential was completely overlooked at first. Only after a thorough search was Samuel able to recognize him as God's choice.

When looking for leaders, do not make hasty judgments based on outward appearances. There are numerous studies that demonstrate how easily we are misled by a leader's physical appearance. Inward character, though harder to assess, is a better qualifier than outward appearance.

The leaders of the next generation may not resemble the leaders of this generation. Our challenge is to ensure that emerging leaders are not overlooked. God has his eye on next-generation leaders, whether we do or not.

4. Recognizing potential—and helping to bring it out—is one of the most critical roles of leadership.

Led by God, Samuel anointed both Saul and David for leadership. Neither Saul nor David had impressive résumés that indicated their qualifications for national leadership. Both were chosen based on their leadership potential rather than on their impressive records of previous performance.

Effective leaders have the ability to recognize the potential in others. They can perceive—within particular individuals—the seeds of success that will produce fruit if only given the right opportunity.

Some of the indicators of leadership potential include integrity, success in previous responsibilities, relational skills, receptivity to feedback (nondefensiveness), ability to bring out the best in others, eagerness to learn, adaptability, and cultural fit.

5. Retirement need not be the end of a leader's contributions.

Even in retirement, Samuel continued to be of significant service to God and his community. Samuel was still willing to be used, had much to contribute, and was provided by God with continued opportunities to serve.

Albert Mohler refers to the "scandal of retirement" and suggests that it would be more appropriate for leaders to think of "redeployment" rather than "retirement."[5] Men and women of character—even though they may be retired—who are willing to share their wisdom, experiences, and insights will always have opportunity to contribute to the success of younger leaders.[6]

Questions for Leadership Development

1. Who has blessed you for leadership?

2. What emerging leader would benefit from your blessing?

3. In what situations is it appropriate to pursue an opportunity for leadership and in what situations should one wait to be pursued by an opportunity for leadership?

4. How can you and your organization actively seek out emerging leaders?

5. What additional leadership lessons can you identify in the story of Samuel?

The Psalm

Psalm 99 describes the majesty of the great and just God who reigns over all the earth and who hears the leaders of his people, notably Moses, Aaron, and Samuel.

Psalm 99

¹The LORD reigns,
    let the nations tremble;
he sits enthroned between the cherubim,
    let the earth shake.
²Great is the LORD in Zion;
    he is exalted over all the nations.
³Let them praise your great and awesome name—
    he is holy.
⁴The King is mighty, he loves justice—
    you have established equity;
in Jacob you have done
    what is just and right.
⁵Exalt the LORD our God
    and worship at his footstool;
    he is holy.
⁶Moses and Aaron were among his priests,
    Samuel was among those who called on his name;
they called on the LORD
    and he answered them.
⁷He spoke to them from the pillar of cloud;
    they kept his statutes and the decrees he gave them.
⁸LORD our God,
    you answered them;
you were to Israel a forgiving God,
    though you punished their misdeeds.
⁹Exalt the LORD our God
    and worship at his holy mountain,
    for the LORD our God is holy.

TWO

JESSE
ROOTS, STUMPS, SHOOTS, AND FAMILY TREES

The Background

The story of Jesse is told in 1 Samuel 16 and 17. He is also mentioned in Ruth 4:17, 22; 1 Samuel 20:27, 30, 31; 22:7, 8, 9, 13; 25:10; 2 Samuel 20:1; 23:1; 1 Kings 12:16; 1 Chronicles 2:12, 13; 12:18; 29:26; 2 Chronicles 10:16; 11:18; Psalm 72:20; Isaiah 11:1, 10; Matthew 1:5, 6; Luke 3:32; Acts 13:22; Romans 15:12.

The Story

Jesse would never forget the day the old prophet Samuel walked into Bethlehem and scared everyone to death. It was not the first time Samuel had been in town. As judge in Israel, he used to visit every year, since Bethlehem was a regular stop on his circuit. Those visits were expected. But this time Samuel appeared unannounced, leading a heifer. The town elders nervously met him and asked what was going on. He said he had come in peace to make a sacrifice.

Jesse was well known and respected in Bethlehem; both his father Obed and grandfather Boaz had lived there; and his eight sons would only have added to his stature in a culture that valued large families. (He and his boys could have fielded their own baseball team.) But he was still surprised when Samuel specifically invited him and his sons to attend the sacrifice. While Samuel prepared the sacrifice, Jesse rounded up his sons. Smoke was just beginning to rise from the wood when they arrived. Jesse was proud to introduce his sons to Samuel, and even prouder to see that Samuel was interested in them, intently looking each one over, almost measuring them. When Samuel saw Eliab, Jesse's eldest son, he was impressed by his stature and certain that this must be God's choice as Israel's next king. However, God said to Samuel, "Do not consider his appearance or his height, for I have rejected him. The LORD does not look at the things man looks at. People look at the outward appearance, but the LORD looks at the heart" (1 Sam. 16:7). When Jesse presented his second son, Abinadab, God told Samuel, "The LORD has not chosen this one either" (v. 8). This happened again with his third son, Shammah, then his fourth, fifth, sixth, and seventh sons. Finally, Samuel asked if Jesse had any other sons. Jesse told him that David, the youngest, was tending the flock.

David was sent for, and Samuel was insistent on waiting until he arrived. Jesse was again surprised, this time at Samuel's obvious excitement about David, who was not the oldest, nor the tallest, nor the most impressive of Jesse's sons. Samuel's demeanor had changed in an instant. He had found the one for whom he had been looking. He took the horn of oil, poured it over David's head, and anointed him king of Israel.

It would be years before Jesse and his sons realized the full import of what had happened that day in Bethlehem when Samuel came to town, leading a cow.

If Jesse was intrigued the day the prophet Samuel showed interest in David, he was even more intrigued the day King Saul showed interest in David. That day the king's messengers appeared, asking questions about Jesse's youngest son. Did he play the harp well? Was he responsible when he watched the sheep? King Saul, suffering from depression and melancholy, needed a dependable young man, adept at playing the harp, to create a soothing atmosphere with his music. Jesse was a little uncomfortable sending this son, whom Samuel had anointed king, to King Saul. But send him he did, along with gifts for the king—a donkey loaded with bread, a skin of wine, and a young goat. The king was so taken with David's harp playing that he asked Jesse for permission to keep him in his court to play for him whenever he was depressed.

David went back and forth between serving Saul and watching his father's sheep in Bethlehem. One day Jesse sent David with provisions for the three older brothers serving in King Saul's army, which was drawn up against the Philistines in the Valley of Elah. That was the day David killed the giant. And that was the day David's victory resulted in Jesse receiving a lifelong reprieve from paying taxes.

Years later when Saul, insane with jealousy, sought to kill David, David fled to the desert. Worried about the safety of his parents, David went to Mizpah to ask permission from the king of Moab to allow his father, Jesse, and his mother to stay under the Moabite king's royal protection. They stayed there until David's fortunes took a turn for the better.

Centuries later Isaiah prophesied, "A shoot will come up from the stump of Jesse; from his roots a Branch will bear fruit" (Isa. 11:1). One wonders if Jesse could have possibly imagined just how significant his family tree would become.

Leadership Lessons

6. Your lasting legacy may be your children.

We have every reason to believe that Jesse was a good and godly man; but his greatest contribution may have been in providing the kind of home from which God would raise up the greatest king in Israel's history.

William Willimon, former dean of Duke (University) Chapel, writes in *The Last Word* about a young lady whose parents sent her to Duke to go to medical school. Once at school, she had gotten an idea about going to Haiti for three years with a church mission program and teaching kids there. Now she wanted to drop out of medical school to become a missionary. The girl's father called

Willimon, irate, holding him personally responsible for the "ruination" of his daughter.

"Wait a minute," Willimon responded, "didn't you dedicate her to the Lord when she was a baby?" "Well, yes," the father stammered. "Didn't you take her to Sunday school when she was little?" "Well, yes," the father muttered. "Well, there you have it," Willimon said. "She was messed up before we ever got her. The damage was done before she ever set foot in our chapel. Congratulations, Mr. Jones, you just helped God make a missionary."[1]

May God bless parents who provide a climate in which it is easy for children to hear, recognize, and respond to God's call on their lives.

7. The one who best knows your past may least know your future.

No one knew David's past better than his father, Jesse. But when it came to David's promising future, Jesse was completely surprised. An axiom of identifying effective leaders is that "past performance predicts future performance." While this adage is valuable in predicting performance in similar situations, it is not effective in determining the type of responsibility for which a leader is best suited. Jesse saw David as a responsible shepherd but had difficulty thinking of David as a potential king.

Be careful not to let past roles limit a person's future potential. Recognizing potential—and helping to bring it out—is one of the most critical roles for leaders.

8. Leaders make people nervous.[2]

Although Samuel was respected and loved by the people of Israel, his unannounced arrival made people nervous—they wondered why he was there.

True leaders have the tendency to make people nervous. It is the sense of a leader's "purposeful presence" that can cause anxiety in others. Leaders do not just show up by accident. They show up at a particular time, in a particular place, for a particular reason. There is a purposefulness to a leader's presence. When the purpose of a leader's presence is unknown, it can cause angst, much like what happened in Bethlehem the day Samuel showed up unexpectedly.

True leaders make people nervous because of the questions they ask when they arrive. The questions often bring pain to the organization, but they are questions that are unavoidable if the organization is going to succeed in achieving its mission.

True leaders can also make people nervous because of the high expectations they bring to an organization—expectations that call for changes in behavior and attitudes. When Samuel became aware of the angst caused by his presence, he allayed the fears of the residents of Bethlehem. Most of the time, leaders will want to lessen any anxiety their presence is causing. On rare occasions—such as when immediate change is necessary to avoid a crisis—leaders may want to take advantage of anxiety caused by their presence in order to initiate corrective action.

Questions for Leadership Development

1. If you could determine your legacy, what would it be?

2. How can a leader avoid underestimating a person's potential?

3. What are the questions you should be asking your organization?

4. What other leadership lessons can be derived from the story of Jesse?

The Psalm

Jesse is specifically mentioned at the end of Psalm 72, a reminder of David's heritage and Jesse's legacy.

Psalm 72

Of Solomon.

¹Endow the king with your justice, O God,
the royal son with your righteousness.
²May he judge your people in righteousness,
your afflicted ones with justice.
³May the mountains bring prosperity to the people,
the hills the fruit of righteousness.
⁴May he defend the afflicted among the people
and save the children of the needy;
may he crush the oppressor.
⁵May he endure as long as the sun,
as long as the moon, through all generations.
⁶May he be like rain falling on a mown field,
like showers watering the earth.
⁷In his days may the righteous flourish
and prosperity abound till the moon is no more.
⁸May he rule from sea to sea
and from the River to the ends of the earth.
⁹May the desert tribes bow before him
and his enemies lick the dust.
¹⁰May the kings of Tarshish and of distant shores
bring tribute to him.
May the kings of Sheba and Seba
present him gifts.
¹¹May all kings bow down to him
and all nations serve him.
¹²For he will deliver the needy who cry out,
the afflicted who have no one to help.
¹³He will take pity on the weak and the needy
and save the needy from death.

[14]He will rescue them from oppression and violence,
    for precious is their blood in his sight.
[15]Long may he live!
    May gold from Sheba be given him.
  May people ever pray for him
    and bless him all day long.
[16]May grain abound throughout the land;
    on the tops of the hills may it sway.
  May the crops flourish like Lebanon
    and thrive like the grass of the field.
[17]May his name endure forever;
    may it continue as long as the sun.
  Then all nations will be blessed through him,
    and they will call him blessed.
[18]Praise be to the LORD God, the God of Israel,
    who alone does marvelous deeds.
[19]Praise be to his glorious name forever;
    may the whole earth be filled with his glory.
        Amen and Amen.
[20]This concludes the prayers of David son of Jesse.

THREE

ELIAB
A BAND OF BROTHERS GIVES WAY TO SIBLING RIVALRY

The Background

The story of Eliab is told in 1 Samuel 16:6; 17:13, 28. He is also mentioned in 1 Chronicles 2:13; 27:18[1]; 2 Chronicles 11:18.

The Story

Much has been written about the qualities and characteristics of firstborns and their inclination toward responsibility and leadership. In his culture, Eliab, as firstborn, was heir to a position of respect and privilege. With the following births of seven brothers, his stock would have only grown. Eliab was accustomed to leading the way. He was a pioneer—the first of his siblings to skip a stone, draw a bow, shear a sheep, or put on a uniform.

Of all of Jesse's sons, Eliab was the one whose appearance was most kingly. He was tall and impressive, much like Saul. When Samuel first saw Eliab, he was certain that the handsome, commanding son of Jesse standing before him would be the next king of Israel. Samuel was mistaken. While Samuel was confident Eliab measured up on the outside, God, who looks at the heart, determined Eliab did not pass muster on the inside.

Eliab could tell by the way Samuel looked at him that he was being considered for the position of king. He would have been very surprised when Samuel poured the horn of oil over the head of David, who in Eliab's eyes must have been seen as inferior. The other six brothers could not have been far behind Eliab in their disbelief.

David was not even a leader in his own family. Such is the plight of the youngest sibling, who seldom has opportunity to practice leadership at home. When you are the youngest, your lot is to follow. On whom do you practice leadership when you are the youngest? If you are David, you practice leadership while tending sheep.

One day Jesse asked David to take provisions to his three oldest brothers serving in Saul's army. Jesse could have sent any of his five sons remaining at home to go to the battle lines, but he sent David to see how Eliab, Abinadab, and Shammah were faring. Jesse may have feared that his other four sons, older than David, would be recruited to join Saul's army. Since David was too young to be pressed into service, he was the one sent with thirty-five pounds of roasted grain and ten loaves of bread for his brothers, and ten cheeses for their commander.

The next morning David, careful to leave the flock under his charge in the care of another shepherd, made his way to the Valley of Elah, where the Philistine and Israelite armies faced each other. David left the provisions with the keeper of supplies and ran to the front lines to check on his brothers.

He arrived in time to hear the army shouting the war cry while taking battle positions, and then he observed the spectacle that had taken place the last forty mornings. Goliath, champion of the Philistines, was challenging Israel's army. David could not believe what he was hearing and seeing. "Is someone going to do something about this Philistine?" he asked. Some Israelite soldiers told David how Saul had promised that the man who killed Goliath would receive great wealth, the hand of the king's daughter in marriage, and an exemption from taxes.

When he heard David speaking with the soldiers, Eliab's resentment, bitterness, and anger erupted. He was furious with David for even thinking he, a shepherd, could fight the giant. Instead of thanking David for delivering the care package, he viciously criticized him.

Though David's intentions were honorable, Eliab first questioned his motives: "Why did you come down here?" Then, though David's heart was pure, Eliab accused David of impudence: "I know your pride and the insolence of your heart" (1 Sam. 17:28, NKJV). Next, though David had been careful to provide for the care of the sheep in his absence, Eliab accused David of irresponsibility: "You have deserted the sheep." Finally, though David was willing to do battle with the giant, Eliab accused him of passive spectatorship: "You are just here to watch the show."[2] It is ironic that for forty days Eliab had been the kind of spectator he accused David of being. The entire Israeli army had watched fearfully as the giant from Gath daily insulted the Israelite army and their God.

It was at that point that David made one of the most important decisions of his life: he turned away from Eliab and started talking to someone else. And that is the last time the words of Eliab are recorded in the Bible.

We do not know what exactly became of Eliab after that day. But one doubts that Eliab ever again questioned David's maturity, responsibility, or bravery. That day, in the Valley of Elah, those questions were forever put to rest.

Leadership Lessons

9. Leadership is a matter of the heart.

Eliab was appealing in his outward appearance and favorably impressed Samuel at first look, but he was not the Lord's anointed. Tall, dark, and handsome are external traits that, though easy to assess, are not qualifications for leadership. What impresses people may not necessarily impress God, who looks at the heart.

The essence of leadership is found on the inside of a person, not on the outside. Eliab was rejected because of his heart. David was chosen because of his heart—a heart God said was after his very own.[3]

10. Nothing reveals your heart like your response to the promotions of others.

David's promotion from shepherd to king had a profound effect on some of his relationships, especially his relationship with his oldest brother. It may very well be that Eliab's unprocessed anger had been smoldering since the day Samuel anointed David rather than him.

When someone else is promoted over you, the motives of your heart will be exposed, be they good or bad. You will either rejoice in the person's success or you will become jealous, as Eliab became with David. We do not see people as they are, but rather as we are.

A leader with a godly heart will be the kind of person who rejoices with those who experience God's blessings and favor.[4] When you are secure in what God is doing in your life, you can praise him for how he is blessing the lives of others. This should be especially true when God favors a family member or friend.

11. Leadership is not spectatorship.

David, unlike Eliab and the rest of Saul's army, was not willing to remain a spectator. David was ready to take action and engage the giant in battle. In the case of the Israelite soldiers, fear had led to paralysis—a common condition on the battlefield. Real fear often reveals aspects of our character that we can otherwise conceal. David was willing to get into the fight, not because of his confidence in himself, but because of his confidence in God.

Leaders act. They are not content to stay on the sidelines. They are willing to take a risk for the King and for the kingdom.

12. Leaders are not derailed by criticism.

Before David could overcome the giant, he had to overcome the criticisms of his own brother. David refused to let Eliab's accusations keep him from taking action. He refused to make a giant out of a criticizer.

Criticism can have a debilitating effect. You may have encountered someone like Eliab—a person full of anger and bitterness who seeks to degrade you and make you feel inferior. Criticism from anyone is difficult to take. It is especially difficult and painful if it is coming from a brother or sister. It is best to respond to criticism with actions above reproach.

One of the most encouraging verses in the Scriptures is Joshua 10:21 (TM), "There was no criticism that day from the People of Israel!" Unfortunately, those days are few and far between. Do not let undue criticism paralyze you and make you inactive. Do not make a giant out of a criticizer.

13. Effective leadership and servanthood are inseparable.

Authority is not the same thing as leadership. The currency of authority is power. The arena of authority is position. The perk of authority is privilege. The currency of leadership is influence. The arena of leadership is servanthood. The perk of leadership is significance.

Eliab had a "position"—he was the eldest son. His was a position of privilege. David did not have a position—he had a "place." It was a place of service. We see David willingly serving his father, serving his brothers, serving the nation, and serving God.

When people seek out a position of authority, it is usually for the perceived benefits associated with the position. Positions of leadership, on the other hand, are almost always sacrificial.

Questions for Leadership Development

1. What characteristics of the heart best qualify a person for leadership?

2. What is your usual reaction to criticism?

3. Would those you serve say you are more prone to offer criticism or encouragement?

4. What other leadership lessons can be derived from the story of Eliab?

The Psalm

Psalm 133 (NASB) is a song of ascents in which David delights in the blessing of harmony and accord among brothers.

Psalm 133

A song of ascents. Of David.

[1]Behold, how good and how pleasant it is
 For brothers to dwell together in unity!
[2]It is like the precious oil upon the head,
 Coming down upon the beard,
 Even Aaron's beard,
 Coming down upon the edge of his robes.
[3]It is like the dew of Hermon
 Coming down upon the mountains of Zion;
 For there the Lord commanded the blessing—life forever.

— FOUR —

GOLIATH
GIANT CHALLENGES ARE GIANT OPPORTUNITIES

The Background

The story of Goliath is told in 1 Samuel 17. He is also mentioned in 1 Samuel 21:9; 22:10; 2 Samuel 21:19; 1 Chronicles 20:5.

The Story

Goliath was the most formidable weapon the Philistines had in their arsenal. A cross between an ogre and a Sherman tank, he was the undefeated combat champion of the Philistine army. With nearly ten feet of brute force, Goliath was tall, dark, and gruesome. His skill at the art of relentless intimidation had been honed to a razor-like edge. The armor and weapons he carried weighed more than most men. Almost every exposed area was covered with bronze. Goliath was outfitted with a bronze helmet, a bronze coat of scale armor weighing 125 pounds, bronze greaves on his legs, and a bronze javelin slung on his back. In one hand he held a spear with a shaft like a telephone pole tipped with a fire hydrant. In the other hand he wielded a sword that resembled a steel surfboard with a handle. His shield bearer went ahead of him lugging what looked like a manhole cover. If you can imagine how the World War I infantryman felt the first time he saw a tank rolling across the trenches in his direction, you can imagine how the Israelites felt the first time they saw Goliath.

Every morning and evening for forty days Goliath bellowed a challenge, lumbering back and forth in the no man's land between the two armies. He taunted Israel, daring them to send a man out to fight, "winner take all." At his challenge knees went weak and hearts melted. Everyone was afraid of Goliath. He seemed invincible. Not even King Saul, the tallest man in Israel, would step out to fight the giant.

Before David ever faced Goliath, he had to overcome two other challenges. The first was the criticism of his brother, Eliab, who told David, "You are too immature to make a difference." Eliab misinterpreted David's confidence in God as arrogance and conceit. He thought David was just "talking big" for the boys, and it angered him. He saw a little brother who was only good enough to tend the sheep in their father's pasture, and who was usurping Eliab's place as the eldest son. Eliab did not know that while David was serving faithfully in the position of a lowly shepherd boy, God was training him to be a giant killer.

David faced a second challenge—the low estimation of King Saul, who told David, "You are too inexperienced to make a difference." After some persuasion, King Saul finally agreed to let David fight the giant when David told the king of how he had overcome a lion and a bear who had threatened the sheep under his care, and that the God who had delivered him from the lion and the bear would deliver him from the giant. Saul then offered David his armor, but David found it cumbersome and declined to wear it. The weapons in David's hand as he approached the giant were a staff, a sling, and five smooth stones he stopped to pick up near the brook that ran between the two armies.

At first, Goliath was dumbfounded when he saw the scantily clad shepherd boy approaching him; but his surprise turned quickly to anger. The Israelites were sending a boy to fight him? Was this a trick? Was this a joke? In Goliath's mind there was no doubt that he was going to kill David. He had faced far more formidable foes. The only question was *how* he was going to kill David. Would he use the spear, the sword, the javelin, or his bare hands? Goliath cursed David, bellowing out a promise to make bird feed out of him, telling David, "You are too insignificant to make a difference."

David replied that his only weapon was the good name of the God he served, and that when God delivered the giant into his hands, he would cut off the giant's head. The battle was the Lord's.

As Goliath moved in for the kill, David slung a stone that sank into Goliath's skull, dropping him quickly. When Goliath "hit the dirt," Frederick Buechner writes, "windows rattled in their frames as far away as Ashkelon."[1] David then took Goliath's sword and cut off his head. When the Philistines saw that their hero was dead, they turned and fled, with Israel in pursuit, killing them and plundering their camp. In the midst of the rout, Saul turned to Joab and asked, "Who is the father of this boy?"[2]

Although the shepherd of sheep would face many more challenges before he became the shepherd of Israel, David's victory over Goliath set the stage for his ultimate ascent to the throne.

Leadership Lessons

14. Leaders prove their capacity to be faithful in the big challenges by being faithful in the little challenges.

If you are faithful in the little things, such as protecting sheep, it is more likely that you will be faithful in the big things, such as facing giants. David's bravery in battling the bear and the lion was evidence of his capacity for bravery when battling the giant.

Faithfulness in small responsibilities is the prerequisite for larger opportunities. David had proven his faithfulness as a shepherd, by both providing for and protecting the flock that was under his care. Charles Swindoll writes, "God's promotions are usually sudden and surprising, so be ready."[3] While promotions from shepherd to king seldom happen, promotions to opportunities with more responsibility occur all the time. Seldom do those promotions occur unless the individual has been faithful in present responsibilities. "It's in the little things and in the lonely places that we prove ourselves capable of the big things."[4] As Swindoll reminds those of us who are pastors, "The test of my calling is not how well I do before the public on Sunday; it is how carefully I cover the bases Monday through Saturday when there is nobody to check up on me, when nobody is looking."[5]

What you do when you are alone and no one is watching prepares you for what you will do when the crowds are watching.

15. Learn to face challenges with the unique weapons and armor with which God has gifted you.

David chose not to wear the king's armor because it felt cumbersome and unfamiliar. He was more comfortable with his simple slingshot, a weapon he was skilled at using. God will use the unique skills he has already placed in your hands. Do not worry about "wearing the king's armor." Just be yourself and use the familiar gifts, skills, tools, and passion God has given you. Face life's challenges with your own gifts. Fight life's battles in your own armor.

16. The enemy wants to take you out.

There can be no question that Goliath wanted to destroy David. His enemy wanted to take him out.

This is especially true of leaders and potential leaders.[6] If the enemy can destroy you, he can seriously harm your organization. This is especially true if your life brings glory to God. The New Testament story of Lazarus bears this out. After Jesus raised Lazarus from the dead, Lazarus's testimony was bringing much glory to God. "So the chief priests made plans to kill Lazarus as well, for on account of him many of the Jews were going over to Jesus" (John 12:10-11). Just like Goliath wanted to take David out, the chief priests wanted to take Lazarus out.

Sometimes the enemy uses a sword or a spear; sometimes the enemy uses temptation or carelessness. If your life brings glory to God, the enemy wants to take you out.

17. Leaders face challenges with courage and confidence in God.

Before he ever faced Goliath, David faced the bear and the lion, and prevailed because of his faith in the power of God. These victories gave him an even greater confidence in God to uphold him through anything that might come his way. It is possible to overcome superior odds with faith, courage, and skill, but faith in God is the irreplaceable ingredient.

Self-confidence alone will ultimately fail and leave you side-lined. God-confidence will keep you in the fight. When leaders walk with God, the bigger the challenge, the bigger the victory.

Questions for Leadership Development

1. What giant problem or impossible situation are you facing that you need God's help to overcome?

2. What are the gifts (weapons) and abilities (armor) God has given you to accomplish the task before you?

3. What courageous action do you need to take, despite potential insults and fearful circumstances?

4. Are you ever tempted to lead like Goliath—from a position of strength, power, and intimidation?

5. What other leadership lessons can be derived from the story of Goliath?

The Psalm

It may be that David wrote Psalm 27 soon after he killed Goliath.

Psalm 27

Of David.

¹The LORD is my light and my salvation—
   whom shall I fear?
The LORD is the stronghold of my life—
   of whom shall I be afraid?
²When the wicked advance against me
   to devour me,
it is my enemies and my foes
   who will stumble and fall.
³Though an army besiege me,
   my heart will not fear;
though war break out against me,
   even then I will be confident.
⁴One thing I ask from the LORD,
   this only do I seek:
that I may dwell in the house of the LORD
   all the days of my life,
to gaze on the beauty of the LORD
   and to seek him in his temple.
⁵For in the day of trouble
   he will keep me safe in his dwelling;
he will hide me in the shelter of his sacred tent
   and set me high upon a rock.
⁶Then my head will be exalted
   above the enemies who surround me;
at his sacred tent I will sacrifice with shouts of joy;
   I will sing and make music to the LORD.
⁷Hear my voice when I call, LORD;
   be merciful to me and answer me.
⁸My heart says of you, "Seek his face!"
   Your face, LORD, I will seek.

⁹Do not hide your face from me,
        do not turn your servant away in anger;
        you have been my helper.
    Do not reject me or forsake me,
        God my Savior.
¹⁰Though my father and mother forsake me,
        the LORD will receive me.
¹¹Teach me your way, LORD;
        lead me in a straight path
        because of my oppressors.
¹²Do not turn me over to the desire of my foes,
        for false witnesses rise up against me,
        spouting malicious accusations.
¹³I remain confident of this:
        I will see the goodness of the LORD
        in the land of the living.
¹⁴Wait for the LORD;
        be strong and take heart
        and wait for the LORD.

FIVE

MICHAL

THE DIFFERENCE BETWEEN A TREASURE AND A TROPHY

The Background

The story of Michal is told in 1 Samuel 18; 19; 25:44; 2 Samuel 3:13-16; 6:15-23. She is also mentioned in 1 Samuel 14:49; 1 Chronicles 15:29.

The Story

Michal was the younger of Saul's two daughters. Her older sister was Merab, and her brothers were Jonathan, Malki-Shua, Abinadab, and Ish-Bosheth. Michal's mother was Ahinoam.

Saul had promised to give his daughter in marriage to whoever killed Goliath. When the time came for Merab to be given in marriage to David, Saul gave her instead to Adriel of Meholah. When Michal fell in love with David, Saul was greatly pleased, for he believed she would be a snare to David. As though killing Goliath was not enough evidence of David's prowess as a warrior, the dowry that Saul demanded for Michal was one hundred foreskins from Philistine warriors. Because circumcision was evidence of the Hebrew covenant with God, foreskins would prove that David had killed Philistines and not males from one of the Israelite tribes. Saul was hoping David would be killed by the Philistines in the attempt. When David brought back not one hundred, but two hundred Philistine foreskins, Saul had no choice but to give Michal in marriage to David.

One night, in a jealous rage, Saul hurled a spear at David. In the melee that followed, David fled to the home that he and Michal shared. When Saul made another attempt to take David's life, this time by sending men to David's house to kill him, Michal warned David and helped him escape through a window. She then deceived Saul and his men by claiming David was ill and confined to bed. To complete the ruse, she put a statue of a household idol in David's bed, covering it with a blanket and topping it with a net of goat's hair. When Saul asked her why she had deceived him, she replied that David had threatened to kill her.

After David's escape, as far as Saul was concerned, Michal's marriage was now null and void, and she could be married off to someone else—someone who would be an ally, not a threat. Saul settled on a man called Paltiel, from the city of Gallim; and the two remained married throughout David's exile.

Following the death of Saul, however, when Abner began negotiations with David about the unification of the kingdom, David remembered his first wife, and made only one demand of both Abner and the new king, Saul's son Ish-Bosheth: that Abner bring Michal with him when he came to see David. Fearing the combined might of David and Abner, Ish-Bosheth gave the order and had Michal taken away from her husband, Paltiel. What follows is one of the most touching, emotionally distressing verses of the Bible.

Paltiel, grief-stricken at the thought of losing his wife, "went with her, weeping behind her all the way to Bahurim" (2 Sam. 3:16). The pathetic, brokenhearted figure followed Michal's entourage along the road for miles, until he was threatened by Ish-Bosheth's general, Abner. Only then did Paltiel relinquish Michal, and she was handed over to David.

It is not known whether David wanted Michal returned because he loved her, because she would strengthen his claim to the throne, or because he simply felt she had been wrongly taken from him. Nor is anything stated of Michal's feelings in the matter.

The next time Michal is mentioned, it becomes apparent that she and David are not enjoying a healthy relationship. When the ark of the covenant was brought into Jerusalem, Michal watched the proceedings from a window. As David led the procession into the city, Michal saw her royal husband leaping, dancing, and whirling in ecstasy before the Lord, wearing only an ephod, showing his near naked body to women and men alike. Aghast, Michal watched the spectacle, and she despised David in her heart. When David returned home from the worship to bless his own home as he had blessed the nation, a furious Michal dressed him down, rebuking David for his behavior and for making himself a spectacle for the admiration of slave girls. David fired back that God had chosen him to be king of Israel over her father, Saul, and that his dancing was religious ecstasy, not sexual vulgarity. This blazing quarrel is the last we see of Michal.

As if to emphasize the deep discord between them, 2 Samuel 6:23 ominously closes Michal's story with this sad report: "And Michal daughter of Saul had no children to the day of her death." In some manuscripts there is reference to Michal having five sons, but evidently Michal raised the children of her sister, Merab.[1] We do not know why Michal had no children of her own. Perhaps David was never again intimate with her.[2] After 2 Samuel 6, Michal disappears from the list of the wives of King David in the Bible.

There is a final postscript to this tragic story. David learned that a three-year famine Israel was experiencing was due to Saul's sin in attempting to annihilate the Gibeonites, in spite of the covenant made between them and Israel.[3] When David approached them to make amends, the Gibeonites requested that seven of Saul's male descendants be given them to be killed. That put David in a very difficult position. He had promised Saul that he would not destroy his house, but this situation was the consequence of Saul's continued rebellion against God. The seven individuals turned over to the Gibeonites included the five sons of Saul's daughter, Merab—the children that Michal had raised. It may be that Michal had already died by this time. If not, the sorrow she would have experienced would have been difficult to bear, and her bitterness toward David would have only increased.

Leadership Lessons

18. Important relationships require time, commitment, and cultivation if they are to be strong and healthy.

The saga of David and Michal is one of the most famous romantic tragedies in the Bible. First Samuel 18:20 states that Michal loved David, the only place in the Bible where a woman's love for a man is recorded. Significantly, there is never any mention of David having loved Michal, as the later story of their marriage seems to imply.

Early in their relationship, Michal clearly loved David with a loyalty that surpassed the love and loyalty she had for her father. When forced to choose between Saul and David, Michal chose David. But in time, Michal grew to despise David in her heart, because David was unwilling to devote the necessary time and commitment needed to nurture his relationship with her.

Michal may have been David's first wife, but she was not his first love. She may have been his trophy for slaying Goliath, but unfortunately she was not his treasure.

Michal may have expected that after Saul's anger had subsided, David would come back to her or at least that he would send for her. But David became a fugitive, living in the backcountry with his ragtag band of soldiers. Perhaps he felt that a royal princess, even though she was his wife, would have been an encumbrance. David was away from Michal for between ten and fourteen years. The months passed, and then the years, and there was no word from him. During that time he built himself a family. Michal eventually heard the bitter news that David had taken another wife, Ahinoam of Jezreel, and then a third, Abigail the widow of Nabal. Michal found herself married to another man, and as the years passed, she probably began to feel her love for David slowly grow cold and die.

Michal had protected David and risked her own life to save him, and in return he had abandoned her. She waited on David, but he never returned, nor did he send for her. David found time to build an army of mighty men. He found time to relate to his close friend, Jonathan (Michal's brother). But when it came to his relationship with Michal, time was not to be found. One wonders how many of David's other relationships were treated in the same way.[4]

Absence does not necessarily make the heart grow fonder. In order for relationships to grow, they must be nurtured. Time and commitment are needed to cultivate healthy relationships.

19. Bitterness can result in barrenness.

Michal was caught in a family feud. She was used as a pawn, first by her father, King Saul, and then by her husband, King David. The love that brought the couple together was replaced by resentment and bitterness. Affection, if not returned, can become disdain. Love, if not nurtured, can develop into contempt. Over time, Michal's love for David turned into scorn. It is unfortunate when this is evidenced in any relationship. It is especially unfortunate when this is evidenced in marriages.

When Michal was given in marriage to Paltiel, she may have found the affection and attention that she had desired. From all appearances, it was a contented marriage—it certainly lacked the drama of her marriage to David—and as the years passed, her disappointment may have faded along with any lingering affection she might have held for David. Then David had Michal wrested away from Paltiel and returned to him. But David's relationship with Michal was apparently not one of love and affection, and no children were born of their union.

When David worshipped with abandon as the ark was brought into Jerusalem, Michal was appalled at David's apparent lack of dignity and decorum. Michal was not only the wife of a king but also the daughter of a king—a princess. She knew how royalty was to behave, and in her opinion David was not living up to his high position. David's unusual behavior may have endeared him to some constituencies, but it further alienated him from Michal. Her bitter sarcasm—"How the king of Israel has distinguished himself today" (2 Sam. 6:20)—elicited a strong response from David, and his true feelings came out as well.

When the Bible states that Michal was barren until her death, it was not just stating a biological condition. In life, and in leadership, the link between attitudes and fruitfulness is easily seen. Bitterness often leads to barrenness, which in turn leads to more bitterness. Thus, a vicious cycle ensues. Bad attitudes often result in a loss of fruitfulness. Engagement, commitment, and passion provide fertile soil for the growth of everything from ideas to relationships. When that fertile soil is absent, fruitfulness is often missing as well.

Questions for Leadership Development

1. How can you best cultivate the important relationships in your life?

2. Do your attitudes tend to result in barrenness or fruitfulness?

3. In what instances have you been tempted to treat those close to you as possessions to be used rather than as people to be valued?

4. What other leadership lessons can be learned from the story of Michal?

The Psalm

In Psalm 59 David writes of his escape after Saul had sent men to watch David's house in order to kill him.

Psalm 59

Of David.

¹Deliver me from my enemies, O God;
    be my fortress against those who are attacking me.
²Deliver me from evildoers
    and save me from those who are after my blood.
³See how they lie in wait for me!
    Fierce men conspire against me
    for no offense or sin of mine, LORD.
⁴I have done no wrong, yet they are ready to attack me.
    Arise to help me; look on my plight!
⁵You, LORD God Almighty,
    you who are the God of Israel,
  rouse yourself to punish all the nations;
    show no mercy to wicked traitors.
⁶They return at evening,
    snarling like dogs,
    and prowl about the city.
⁷See what they spew from their mouths—
    the words from their lips are sharp as swords,
    and they think, "Who can hear us?"
⁸But you laugh at them, LORD;
    you scoff at all those nations.
⁹You are my strength, I watch for you;
    you, God, are my fortress,
    ¹⁰my God on whom I can rely.
  God will go before me
    and will let me gloat over those who slander me.
¹¹But do not kill them, Lord our shield,
    or my people will forget.

In your might uproot them
  and bring them down.
¹²For the sins of their mouths,
    for the words of their lips,
    let them be caught in their pride.
  For the curses and lies they utter,
¹³   consume them in your wrath,
    consume them till they are no more.
  Then it will be known to the ends of the earth
    that God rules over Jacob.
¹⁴They return at evening,
    snarling like dogs,
    and prowl about the city.
¹⁵They wander about for food
    and howl if not satisfied.
¹⁶But I will sing of your strength,
    in the morning I will sing of your love;
  for you are my fortress,
    my refuge in times of trouble.
¹⁷You are my strength, I sing praise to you;
    you, God, are my fortress,
    my God on whom I can rely.

— SIX —

JONATHAN

THE BLESSING OF A COVENANT FRIEND

The Background

The story of Jonathan is told in 1 Samuel 13; 14; 18:1-4; 19:1-7; 20; 23:16-18; 31:2; 2 Samuel 1; 21:12-14. He is also mentioned in 2 Samuel 4:4; 9:1-7; 21:7; 1 Chronicles 8:33-34; 9:39-40; 10:2.

The Story

Perhaps the greatest friendship in Scripture is the friendship of David and Jonathan. Jonathan was the oldest son of King Saul and Ahinoam, and heir to his father's throne.

Before he ever met David, Jonathan was already a daring and successful young officer in Saul's army. Jonathan's first recorded exploit is the attack on the Philistines at Geba. Two thousand Israelites were under the king's command at Mikmash, while Jonathan led a thousand men to victory against the outpost at Geba. The Philistines reacted swiftly, sending a strong force back into the hills to occupy Mikmash.

Saul was forced to fall back to Gilgal with a greatly reduced army—now numbering only six hundred men—the rest having fled in fear. Jonathan and Saul were the only two soldiers in Israel's army with a sword or a spear. The rest of the army had only farming implements as weapons. In spite of this desperate situation, Jonathan, accompanied only by his armor-bearer, slipped away from Saul and his men and set off on a covert mission. They climbed up a rocky pass and surprised the Philistine outpost at Mikmash, killing twenty men in a commando attack. The resulting panic spread to the main camp, and soon the Philistines were in headlong flight.

Saul's scouts observed the Philistine retreat, and it was soon discovered that Jonathan and his armor-bearer were missing from the Israelite camp. At that point, Saul and his men joined the fight and found the Philistines attacking each other in confusion. Victory would have been complete if Saul had not strangely ordered the soldiers to refrain from eating until the end of the day. Unaware of the prohibition, Jonathan, in hot pursuit of the enemy, refreshed himself by eating some wild honey found on the ground, which immediately renewed his strength. Saul decreed that Jonathan must die for disobeying orders, but the army rose up in Jonathan's defense and Saul relented.

As great as Jonathan's military qualities were, he is best remembered for his friendship with David. Their relationship began the day David killed Goliath, when Jonathan impulsively presented David with the gift of his clothing and weapons. At once the two were kindred spirits, and the affection between them was strong.

Not long after, Jonathan warned David when a jealous Saul made plans to have David killed. Jonathan went to his father and spoke on David's behalf, reminding Saul of the many ways David had benefitted the king. Saul changed his mind, and David was safe for a time. However, it was not long before Saul tried to pin David to the wall with a spear. When the attempt failed, he sent a squad of soldiers to assassinate David in his home, but David escaped with the help of his wife, Michal, who was also Jonathan's sister.

David soon made his way to Jonathan again, trying to discern why Saul wanted to kill him. Jonathan assured David that the king would certainly take his own son into his confidence in such a matter, but that he had not done so. David was convinced that Saul wanted to kill him, though, and replied that Saul had not shared his plans because he knew that such news would distress Jonathan.

The two of them devised a way to be certain of Saul's intention. David was expected to dine with the king at the annual celebration of the New Moon feast. If his absence, which would be conspicuous, resulted in King Saul losing his temper, then they would know that the king had murder on his mind. If the king responded gracefully to the absence, they would know David was safe. They agreed to meet in two days in a large field with a boulder where Jonathan would signal David by shooting arrows.

The first day of the feast, when David's place was empty, the king said nothing. The second day of the feast, when David was again missing, Saul asked Jonathan why David was absent. Jonathan explained that David had requested permission to miss the feast in order to participate with his brothers in a sacrifice taking place in Bethlehem. Saul became violently angry, shouting insults at Jonathan, and ordering that David be killed in order to save the throne for Jonathan. When Jonathan tried to reason with his father, Saul angrily picked up a spear and hurled it at him. Having narrowly escaped death himself, Jonathan hastily left the feast.

The next morning Jonathan went out to the field and shot his arrows, just as he had promised he would do. He called out to his young helper, "The arrow went far beyond you! Hurry, run fast!" This was the signal to David that Saul wanted to kill him. The boy retrieved his arrows, and Jonathan sent him home. Then David came out from behind the boulder. The two friends embraced, wept together, and swore eternal loyalty.

Later, while David was on the run from Saul and his soldiers, Jonathan met David at Horesh. Although Saul and his troops could not locate David, Jonathan had no difficulty. Jonathan encouraged his friend, strengthened him in God, and predicted that David would become king. He pledged David his complete support and expressed his willingness to be second to David. This would be the last meeting between David and Jonathan.

Jonathan, his father King Saul, and his brothers, Abinadab and Malki-Shua, were killed in the defeat of the Israelite army by the Philistines on Mount Gilboa. Their bodies were mutilated and hung on the wall of Beth Shan, a nearby city. The citizens of Jabesh Gilead, out of gratitude for what Saul had done for them at the beginning of his career, recovered the bodies under cover of night and gave them honorable burial. David, still in exile, poured his anguish into a lament for his beloved friend.[1] David later had the bones of Saul and Jonathan buried in the tomb of Saul's father, Kish, at Zela.

Jonathan was the father of Mephibosheth, to whom David would show great kindness.

Leadership Lessons

20. A covenant friendship is a special kind of relationship.

A covenant friendship is the solemn promise of friendship between two people. The relationship between David and Jonathan is a good example of a covenant friendship. Young David found in Jonathan someone who was more than just a friend. Their relationship is perhaps the most profound friendship described in the Bible.

The Bible records three covenants made between Jonathan and David. The first covenant was made very shortly after they met, when Jonathan gave David his robe, tunic, sword, bow, and belt.[2] The robe represented Jonathan's stature, his rank, his place of leadership. The tunic and belt represented Jonathan's material possessions. The sword would have been a magnificent gift, representing Jonathan's power to wage war and expressing that the power available to Jonathan as Saul's son was now available to David. Under the Philistines, the Israelites were not allowed to have blacksmiths, and there were only two swords in all of Israel. One was owned by Saul, and the other was owned by Jonathan. Now David possessed both Jonathan's sword and Goliath's sword. Jonathan's bow was perhaps his most favorite weapon as it is the weapon most often mentioned in reference to Jonathan. In essence, Jonathan was saying, "Take my possessions. I give you everything of value I have, and I give you the significance attached to each of these items." It is as though Jonathan recognized in David qualifications for the kingship that neither he nor his father, Saul, possessed.

The second covenant was made near the end of their time together in Gibeah and is recorded in 1 Samuel 20:16-17. This was a promise of safety and protection extended by Jonathan to David and his family, and a promise of kindness extended by David to Jonathan and his family.

The third covenant was probably made several years later and is noted in 1 Samuel 23:18. This covenant recognized both that David would become king and that Jonathan would support him and stand by his side in the new reign.

As far as we know, David was the only one to whom Jonathan was such a friend. While there are others, such as Hushai, who are noted as being a friend to David, there are no others with whom David shared such a deep friendship.

While the relationship between Jonathan and David was special, there is no indication that it was sexual. The attempt by some to make their relationship an immoral one is an unfortunate attempt to twist an innocent, platonic relationship into one designed to further a misguided agenda.

Because such a level of friendship bears with it tremendous obligations, a covenant friend should be carefully chosen. Such an intense friendship may be unusual, and perhaps even awkward, in some modern cultures. However, the pledges and promises associated with a covenant friendship make it a source of significant mutual blessings.

Such a friendship need not be marked by a formal ceremony, but it is likely that it will have been carefully and intentionally cultivated over a period of time. It takes time to develop a covenant friendship—time to invest in one another's growth, time to listen, time to care, time to build memories, and time to build trust. Such a friendship will include components such as shared experiences, shared values, and even shared possessions. A friend says, "Anytime you need to borrow my truck, just let me know."

A covenant friend says, "Just in case you need it, here is an extra key to my truck."

21. A covenant friendship is marked by a kindredness of spirit.

There are several characteristics of a covenant relationship that can be a model for strong, healthy friendships today. First, Jonathan and David were kindred spirits, equally brave, equally impulsive, equally convinced that God was behind Israel. They were both leaders of men.

They were kindred spirits in bravery. Jonathan was one of the greatest warriors in the history of Israel. He and his armor-bearer had the courage to attack an entire Philistine garrison by themselves. Undoubtedly, when Jonathan saw David do battle with Goliath, he recognized the kind of bravery that he himself had earlier displayed.

They were close friends whose hearts were knit together by a mutual commitment to faithful friendship. It seems that Jonathan expressed his friendship to David every time he saw him. Again and again he took care to tell David of his love, devotion, and friendship. This is very important in a covenant relationship. It is not often that God knits two hearts together. The person who has a relationship like this is most blessed.

The development of a kindred spirit is most often forged through common experiences and common interests. Nothing ties people together like having gone through the same difficult experience and being impressed with the courage, grace, and strength displayed by the other. We tend to be drawn to people whose character mirrors our own or whose character we admire and desire to emulate. Good character attracts good character.

Kindred spirits may be developed and discovered as two individuals share a bond that joins them—be it fighting the same battle, working on the same challenging project, overcoming similar addictions, playing on the same sports team, or enduring comparable loss.

22. A covenant friendship is marked by loyalty.

A covenant friend is loyal and faithful. Jonathan's loyalty often expressed itself through advocacy and intercession. When Jonathan realized his father's animosity toward David, he interceded for his friend. More than once he risked his life for him. Over and over again, Jonathan defended David before Saul, interceding with the king on David's behalf.

It would have been easy for Jonathan to be jealous of David. After all, this was the man who would one day be king in his place. But Jonathan steadfastly showed loyalty for his covenant friend.

In a covenant friendship there is no backbiting and no room for jealousy. There is no fear that words shared in confidence will end up on the Internet the next day. A great level of trust in each other leads to a great level of confidence in each other.

A covenant friendship can be both challenging and exciting. A loyal friend will take risks for you and love you unconditionally. A loyal friend will tell you the truth, even if you do not want to hear it, if it lies in your best interest. A loyal friend will not lack the mercy to correct you when you are wrong. A loyal friend will stick with you in good times and in bad. That is the meaning of loyalty.

Loyalty—steadfast devotion—is a necessary component of a covenant friendship and a key ingredient in the deepest of healthy relationships.

23. A covenant friendship is marked by encouragement.

A friend has been defined as someone who comes in when everyone else goes out. Jonathan was a great encourager to David. When David was running for his life from King Saul, Jonathan found David and brought him encouragement, strengthening him in the Lord.

I have always appreciated what was said of Job: "Your words have put stumbling people on their feet, put fresh hope in people about to collapse" (Job 4:4, TM). The encouraging words of a covenant friend can cause you to stand when you would have fallen.

Receiving the encouraging support of another on a consistent basis is indicative of a covenant friendship.

Great inspiration can be found in a friend who encourages. Such relationships enable us to be more faithful and more fruitful, to perform our responsibilities better, to live better lives, and to reach our full potential. A true friend leads you to righteousness and enables you to become a better servant of God. Such was the case with Jonathan, and such should be the case with us.

David's son, Solomon, would later write, "As iron sharpens iron, so one person sharpens another" (Prov. 27:17). David and Jonathan kept each other sharp. The presence and influence of each made the other stronger and better.

It is interesting to note what happened to David after Jonathan died. Not long after Jonathan's death, David had his terrible affair with Bathsheba. Then his children were involved in incest, murder, and betrayal. None of this happened to David while he had his friend. Perhaps Jonathan's presence could have made a difference in David's choices later on in life.

24. A covenant friendship is marked by unselfishness.

A true, covenant friend is willing to be second. Jonathan was the heir apparent to the throne, but David's welfare meant more than his own. True love and true friendship knows no bounds of sacrifice, love, and giving.

Jonathan's willingness to surrender all claims to the throne for the sake of his friend gives evidence of his character. True friendship is willing to exalt the other in place of self. True friendship steps in the shadows and pushes the friend into the limelight. True friendship finds its satisfaction in helping rather than in being helped. True friendship rejoices in the success of a friend.

Jonathan was willing to give up worldly glory, and he was willing to risk his very life for the sake of his friend David. He was willing to be such a friend because he trusted God's good intentions for his own life and legacy.

True friendship involves a desire to see one another grow and develop, and a genuine hope for each other to succeed in all areas of life. Such a covenant friend initiates action for the other while expecting nothing in return.

Self-centered individuals rarely are able to focus attention on someone else. But covenant friends ensure that the conversation does not always revolve around themselves and regularly express interest in the life of the other.

It is very rare to *have* such a friend as Jonathan. It is even rarer to desire to *be* a friend like Jonathan.

25. A covenant friendship can bless succeeding generations.

Jonathan and David made a covenant of friendship and peace that was to last through their descendants forever.[3] After David became king, the covenant the two men had formed eventually led to David graciously seating Jonathan's disabled son, Mephibosheth, at his own royal table instead of eradicating the line of the former king.

Just as the sins of an individual can result in negative consequences to the second and third generation, so the blessings of covenant friendship can bear good fruit for succeeding generations. The blessings of your covenant friendship may very well outlive you. Your covenant friendship will provide a model for the next generation that can be lived out again through them. Your deep friendship may also result in inherited blessings for your children and grandchildren through gracious words and kind deeds extended to them by others as a direct result of the legacy of your covenant friendship.

26. Every leader needs a covenant friendship.

A covenant friend is someone who can help you become a better person and a better leader. Such friends are priceless. As a leader, you would do well to identify, nurture, and develop friendships that will build you up, encourage you, and enable you to better navigate hard times.

While it is true that a leader needs to *have* a covenant friend, it is also true that a leader needs to *be* a covenant friend. Not only did David need a covenant friend *in* Jonathan; he needed to be a covenant friend *to* Jonathan. David needed to learn to be loyal, encouraging, and unselfish.

As I count the blessings of my life, I am grateful that the different seasons of my life have been marked by the significant blessing of good friends: Geoff, Ben, Lance, Ron, Jimmy, Tim, Larry, Greg, and Rick. These friends have been answers to prayer.

Do not be afraid to pray that God would bless you with a covenant friendship. God wants to pour out the blessing of friendship on you. A great friend who loves you and encourages you to be godly is a wonderful gift.

Questions for Leadership Development

1. What qualities did David and Jonathan share?

2. Why do you think Jonathan and David thought their friendship important enough to merit a covenant?

3. In what ways could having a covenant friend make you a better leader?

4. Do you have a covenant friend? If so, who is it?

5. Would it be wise for you to pray that God would bless you with a covenant friend?

6. What other leadership lessons can be derived from the story of Jonathan?

The Psalm

Some suggest that Psalm 133 is David's psalm to Jonathan, his covenant friend, and that David likens the pleasantness of their relationship with precious oil and the dew of Mount Hermon.

Psalm 133

A song of ascents. Of David.
¹How good and pleasant it is
    when God's people live together in unity!
²It is like precious oil poured on the head,
    running down on the beard,
  running down on Aaron's beard,
    down on the collar of his robe.
³It is as if the dew of Hermon
    were falling on Mount Zion.
  For there the LORD bestows his blessing,
    even life forevermore.

— SEVEN —

DOEG
A MAN AFTER SAUL'S OWN HEART

The Background

The story of Doeg is told in 1 Samuel 21:1-9; 22:6-23. He is also mentioned in Psalm 52.

The Story

Doeg was Saul's chief shepherd and apparently one of his most vile minions. An Edomite, Doeg was a descendant of Esau. He was a traitor to his own people, for Israel and Edom were enemies.[1]

It was Doeg who observed David and Ahimelek's interaction the day David, now a fugitive on the run from Saul, made his way to the tabernacle in Nob seeking food and a weapon. Ahimelek offered David the consecrated bread, normally reserved for the priests, and the sword of Goliath the Philistine, which apparently had been placed in the tabernacle for safekeeping and as a re-minder of God's blessing. Not long after, Saul learned of David's movements and accused his officials of conspiring against him by not keeping him informed of the actions of Jonathan and Da-vid. Doeg spoke up with the news that he had seen David with Ahimelek at Nob and that Ahimelek had provided David with counsel, provisions, and Goliath's sword. Doeg neglected to in-form Saul that David had deceived Ahimelek by pretending to be on a clandestine mission for the king and that Ahimelek had

65

provided assistance to David because he thought he was doing the king's business. This may be why David blamed Doeg, and not Saul, for what happened next.

Saul angrily summoned Ahimelek and all the priests at Nob. After accusing Ahimelek of treason, Saul ordered that he and the rest of the priests be executed. When Saul's guards respectfully refused to lift a hand against the priests, the king ordered Doeg to carry out the execution, which he did in brutal excess. It was a vendetta of personal vindictiveness. He murdered Ahimelek and eighty-four of his fellow priests, along with all the inhabitants of Nob, women and men, children and infants. With the exception of one survivor, every living thing in Nob was destroyed, even the livestock.

Only Abiathar, son of Ahimelek, escaped with his life. When Abiathar made his way to David to share the news of the massacre, David expressed his regret and voiced responsibility for the death of Ahimelek and his family. He recalled that when he saw Doeg in Nob, he knew Doeg would be sure to tell Saul. Whatever became of Doeg is not told in the Bible. He is only mentioned once again—in Psalm 52—where David makes known his opinion of Doeg's treachery.

Leadership Lessons

27. Your presence in a place of worship does not guarantee that you are a person of worship.

The purpose of Doeg's presence at Nob is unknown. Since he was an Edomite and not a native Israelite, perhaps he was there because he wanted the Israelites to observe his willingness to adopt their religious practices, or to fulfill a vow. The meaning of the phrase "detained before the LORD" (1 Sam. 21:7) may indicate that he was attempting to follow the letter of the law of the Israelites.

You can be in the right place for the wrong reason. While Doeg may have followed an outward form of worship, his heart did not reflect an inner spirit of worship. It is difficult to imagine the kind of heart that motivates a person to murder eighty-five priests and an entire village. He carried out a wicked deed, showing no respect for God's priests and no regard for the lives of the righteous and the innocent.

28. Someone is always looking.

David was aware that he was being observed at Nob, and he had a premonition that Doeg would tell Saul what he had seen and heard. David, "a man after God's own heart,"[2] was betrayed by Doeg, "a man after Saul's own heart."[3]

Of this you can be certain: someone is always looking. It seems that a "Doeg" is often lurking around the corner. Such knowledge should provide forewarning. Your words, and your actions, are observed more than you may realize. Too many leaders ignore this truth, and like David, come to regret it when their actions, and their words are repeated by others in ways that result in regrettable consequences.

29. When leaders deceive—even for good reasons—the negative consequences can prove devastating.

At the time, David may have rationalized that his deception of Ahimelek was harmless. After all, the consecrated bread was old and stale and the sword had been in storage for some time. However, David's deception had tragic consequences. Ahimelek, as well as the entire village of Nob, paid a terrible price for David's lie.

Facing negative consequences for one's honesty is much more honorable than facing negative consequences for one's dishonesty. Telling the truth is a characteristic of moral leadership.

Questions for Leadership Development

1. How can you counteract the evil intentions of someone who is observing you?

2. Can you recall a time when a leader deceived, even for good reasons, and the negative consequences proved devastating?

3. What other leadership lessons can be derived from the story of Doeg?

The Psalm

David wrote an entire psalm about Doeg's evil, expressing his disgust at Doeg's treachery.

Psalm 52

For the director of music. A maskil *of David. When Doeg the Edomite had gone to Saul and told him: "David has gone to the house of Ahimelek."*

¹Why do you boast of evil, you mighty hero?
>Why do you boast all day long,
>>you who are a disgrace in the eyes of God?

²You who practice deceit,
>your tongue plots destruction;
>>it is like a sharpened razor.

³You love evil rather than good,
>falsehood rather than speaking the truth.

⁴You love every harmful word,
>you deceitful tongue!

⁵Surely God will bring you down to everlasting ruin:
>He will snatch you up and pluck you from your tent;
>>he will uproot you from the land of the living.

⁶The righteous will see and fear;
>they will laugh at you, saying,

⁷"Here now is the man
>who did not make God his stronghold
but trusted in his great wealth
>and grew strong by destroying others!"

⁸But I am like an olive tree
>flourishing in the house of God;
I trust in God's unfailing love
>for ever and ever.

⁹For what you have done I will always praise you
>in the presence of your faithful people.
And I will hope in your name,
>for your name is good.

EIGHT

ACHISH
LIVING WITH THE ENEMY

The Background

The story of Achish is told in 1 Samuel 21:10-15; 27:2-12; 28:1-2; 29:1-11. He is also mentioned in 1 Kings 2:39-40.

The Story

After David left Ahimelek at Nob, with food in his belly and a sword in his hand, he fled to Achish, the king of Gath. Gath was the hometown of Goliath and was located in Philistine territory. It was a strange place for David to hide out, but perhaps he thought it was the last place Saul would look for him.

David was incognito, but the servants of Achish recognized David and warned Achish of David's fame. Apparently David's reputation had preceded him, because the servants repeated the song being sung in Israel, "Saul has slain his thousands; and David his tens of thousands" (1 Sam. 18:7). The problem was those "tens of thousands" were Philistines, and David was now in Philistine country. When Achish's servants shared their suspicion of David with Achish, David became fearful. He feigned insanity, madly clawing on the doors of the gates and drooling. David may well have been mimicking the behavior of Saul he had observed many times. Achish was repulsed and dismissed David as a lunatic.

David then fled to the cave of Adullam, where his family, along with four hundred other distressed, in debt, and discontented men, gathered around him. As Saul's relentless pursuit continued, David and his band of renegades managed to stay one step ahead of the murderous king.

David finally grew weary of running from Saul and for a second time he made his way to Philistine country to seek refuge with Achish, knowing Saul would not follow him there. By this time, David's ranks had swollen to six hundred men. Each of David's men had his family with him, and David had his two wives: Ahinoam of Jezreel and Abigail of Carmel, the widow of Nabal. When Saul learned that David had settled in Gath, he ceased searching for David.

David and his men were welcomed by Achish, who supposed that they, too, were now enemies of Saul and would be willing to fight against him as mercenaries. David asked Achish for a country town in which he and his men could dwell, so they would not be an inconvenience to Achish in Gath. Achish gave him Ziklag, and David and his men lived there for sixteen months.

Ziklag became the center of operations for David and his men, from which they would go on raiding forays, wiping out entire villages and plundering livestock and possessions. When Achish asked David where the raids were taking place, David deceived him by indicating the Negev of Judah, Jerahmeel, and the Kenites. In fact, it was the lands of the Geshurites, Girzites, and Amalekites that were being pillaged—tribes hostile to Israel. Since all the inhabitants of the villages David was raiding were killed, there was no one to inform Achish of what David was really doing. Achish believed that David was raiding Israel and had become the enemy of his fellow Israelites.

When it came time for the Philistines to go to battle against Israel, Achish wanted David and his men to accompany him in the Philistine army as his personal protection detail. The Philistine commanders would have nothing of it. Even with assurance from Achish of David's loyalty, they would not allow David and his men to march with them. The suspicious Philistine commanders feared that David would turn against them during battle. They demanded that David and his men be sent back to Ziklag. Achish assured David of his confidence, then regretfully told him of the decision to send David and his men back. The verdict saved David from joining the battle against Israel, King Saul, and Jonathan at Mount Gilboa.

Achish and the Philistine commanders went on to defeat Saul at the battle of Mount Gilboa, where Saul and his sons Jonathan, Abinadab, and Malki-Shua were killed.

Leadership Lessons

30. If you have to pretend to be someone or something you are not, perhaps you are not in the right place.[1]

Gath was Goliath's hometown and a Philistine village, as was Ziklag. David had no business living there, among the enemies of Israel. This is a season of duplicity in David's life. He hides his identity, pretending to be something he is not. Swindoll writes, "David is facing a real identity crisis. He's a displaced person. He's become neither Philistine nor Israelite. Like the carnal Christian, he doesn't feel comfortable in the things of God, but he's now losing interest in his life in the pits. It's a battle for identity."[2]

David was a resourceful and cunning man, and able to think quickly on his feet. But if you find yourself living a lie, you are not living in the right place.

31. For good and for ill, decisions you make affect the lives of others.

When David moved in with the enemy, he did not go alone. He took his troops and their families. Sinful choices have sinful consequences. Swindoll writes, "When you make a decision that is wrong, when you choose a course that is not God's plan, it affects those who trust you and depend on you, those who look up to you and believe in you. Though innocent, they become contaminated by your sinful choices."[3]

The families of David and his men were living unprotected in a land in which they should not have been. When you are where you are not supposed to be, you become easy pickings for the enemy.

32. Our good fortune sometimes has everything to do with God's graceful providence.

Because the Philistine kings refused to let David march with them, David was far from the battle when Saul and his sons were killed on Mount Gilboa. After repeatedly refusing to harm Saul, David could have been blamed for Saul's death, had he been allowed to fight. He may have been disappointed with the decision, but it was ultimately for his good. God protected David from fighting against Saul.

Thank God for his providence, which in each of our lives has at times protected us from the unintentional consequences of our unwise intentions.

Questions for Leadership Development

1. In what ways are leaders sometimes tempted to "live among the enemy"?

2. How can leaders know when they are in the "wrong place"?

3. Why might leaders pretend to be someone they are not?

4. What other leadership lessons can be derived from the story of Achish?

The Psalm

The heading of Psalm 34 makes reference to David's escape when he visited Achish at Gath the first time.[4]

Psalm 34

Of David. When he pretended to be insane before Abimelek, who drove him away, and he left.

¹I will extol the LORD at all times;
    his praise will always be on my lips.
²I will glory in the LORD;
    let the afflicted hear and rejoice.
³Glorify the LORD with me;
    let us exalt his name together.
⁴I sought the LORD, and he answered me;
    he delivered me from all my fears.
⁵Those who look to him are radiant;
    their faces are never covered with shame.
⁶This poor man called, and the LORD heard him;
    he saved him out of all his troubles.
⁷The angel of the LORD encamps around those who fear him,
    and he delivers them.
⁸Taste and see that the LORD is good;
    blessed is the one who takes refuge in him.
⁹Fear the LORD, you his holy people,
    for those who fear him lack nothing.
¹⁰The lions may grow weak and hungry,
    but those who seek the LORD lack no good thing.
¹¹Come, my children, listen to me;
    I will teach you the fear of the LORD.
¹²Whoever of you loves life
    and desires to see many good days,
¹³keep your tongue from evil
    and your lips from telling lies.
¹⁴Turn from evil and do good;
    seek peace and pursue it.

¹⁵The eyes of the LORD are on the righteous,
    and his ears are attentive to their cry;
¹⁶but the face of the LORD is against those who do evil,
    to blot out their name from the earth.
¹⁷The righteous cry out, and the LORD hears them;
    he delivers them from all their troubles.
¹⁸The LORD is close to the brokenhearted
    and saves those who are crushed in spirit.
¹⁹The righteous person may have many troubles,
    but the LORD delivers him from them all;
²⁰he protects all his bones,
    not one of them will be broken.
²¹Evil will slay the wicked;
    the foes of the righteous will be condemned.
²²The LORD will rescue his servants;
    no one who takes refuge in him will be condemned.

NINE

ABIGAIL

BEAUTY AND THE BEAST (PT. 1)

The Background

The story of Abigail is told in 1 Samuel 25. She is also mentioned in 1 Samuel 27:2-4; 30:4-6; 2 Samuel 2:2; 3:3; and 1 Chronicles 3:1.

The Story

Abigail was a beautiful and intelligent Israelite woman. Unfortunately, she was married to Nabal, a wealthy Calebite who owned property in Carmel and Moen and great herds of goats and sheep. But he was a lout and as uncouth as he was rich.

David, mourning the recent death of Samuel, was hiding in the wilderness (desert of Paran) from Saul, who was intent on killing him. While there, David and his men provided protection for Nabal's shepherds and herds in the area. When David learned that Nabal was shearing sheep in Carmel, he sent men to warmly greet Nabal and to request provisions, based on the custom of hospitality and sharing wealth with those who have provided assistance.

Nabal's response was surly and anything but hospitable. He was a jerk. David was livid when his men relayed Nabal's response and he immediately called them to prepare for battle. Four hundred marched out with David to pick a fight in Carmel.

Meanwhile, without Nabal's knowledge, one of the servants told Abigail what had transpired between David's men and Nabal, and how Nabal had treated David's men—hurling insults at them when they had in fact provided a valuable service to him. The servant recognized the probable consequence of Nabal's action—impending disaster—and asked Abigail to do something about it.

Abigail realized she did not have much time. She acted immediately, preparing provisions to take to David, including two hundred loaves of bread, two skins of wine, five dressed sheep, sixty pounds of roasted grain, a hundred cakes of raisins, and two hundred cakes of pressed figs. With Nabal unaware of her actions, she departed, following her servants in a desperate attempt to find David before it was too late.

When Abigail intercepted David and his force, he was well on his way to Carmel, determined to wipe out Nabal and his men. She greeted David, asked him to overlook Nabal's foolishness, and presented him the provisions. She also asked David to spare Nabal's life, not for the sake of saving Nabal, but for the sake of saving David's reputation.

Abigail's creative approach changed David's heart and his mind. David responded to her request with gratitude and grace and sent her home with assurance that he would spare Nabal's life.

Abigail returned home to find Nabal drunkenly hosting a party. The next morning, when he was sober, Abigail told him what had happened. He promptly suffered a heart attack and died ten days later.

When David heard the news, he praised God for bringing Nabal's wrongdoing down on Nabal's own head. Then he proposed to Abigail, and she accepted, becoming David's second wife.

Leadership Lessons

33. It is easy for leaders to overreact to slights, especially when under stress.

David was probably experiencing raw emotions when he suffered Nabal's great affront. Not only was David fleeing from Saul, but he was also mourning the recent death of Samuel. It was easy for him to respond in anger when Nabal offended him. David's initial response was swift and certain: David intended to kill Nabal and all of Nabal's men.[1] Fortunately, Abigail intercepted David and gave him opportunity to consider a more reasoned approach.

Leaders are wise to measure their response to perceived slights, especially when the inclination is to respond quickly and forcefully. Remaining calm and responding with reason during emotionally stressful situations is a skill that can be developed. The development of that skill begins with self-awareness, looking for signs that you are reacting with emotional heat rather than responding with judicious wisdom, and an honest recognition of personal responsibility. The skill can be cultivated through role-playing and by observing and emulating other leaders who successfully navigate volatile situations. When faced with conflict, be wise. Do not act in haste. Consider the consequences, and other perspectives, before responding. Listen to people God may place in your path to caution you. Their wisdom may keep you from taking hasty action you will later regret.

Leaders are most effective when they have a non-anxious presence and the ability to avoid making bad situations worse. A non-defensive posture, response, and attitude allows a leader to keep the focus on solutions to issues rather than becoming part of the issue themselves.

Emotion can be a valuable asset, and often provides the impetus to act appropriately. Emotion need not be jettisoned—only harnessed.

34. The "art of de-escalation" is a valuable skill in defusing a volatile situation.

It has been said that leaders carry two buckets with them: one of water, one of fuel. The art of leadership is to know which bucket to use—the bucket of water to dampen a situation needing to be quenched or the bucket of fuel to further energize a situation. The wise leader will know which bucket is called for in a given situation.

In times of conflict, leaders can recognize which bucket to use by keeping their original goal in mind. For David the original goal was food and respect. Abigail is the true leader in this story because, while Nabal and David are carried away by their own egos and emotions, Abigail used creative initiative to wisely provide David with what he originally sought. Only after diffusing the situation did she remind David of what he would be sacrificing if he murdered Nabal. It may well be that this story prompted Solomon to pen Proverbs 15:1, "A gentle answer turns away wrath, but a harsh word stirs up anger."

Questions for Leadership Development

1. What tools can leaders use to ensure that in times of anger and stress they do not make emotional decisions or take hasty actions that they will regret?

2. How can leaders become proficient in the "art of de-escalation"?

3. What other leadership lessons are derived from the story of Abigail?

The Psalm

Psalm 94:1–15 describes the God who brings justice upon the wicked and the proud.

Psalm 94:1-15

¹The Lord is a God who avenges.
    O God who avenges, shine forth.
²Rise up, Judge of the earth;
    pay back to the proud what they deserve.
³How long, Lord, will the wicked,
    how long will the wicked be jubilant?
⁴They pour out arrogant words;
    all the evildoers are full of boasting.
⁵They crush your people, Lord;
    they oppress your inheritance.
⁶They slay the widow and the foreigner;
    they murder the fatherless.
⁷They say, "The Lord does not see;
    the God of Jacob takes no notice."
⁸Take notice, you senseless ones among the people;
    you fools, when will you become wise?
⁹Does he who fashioned the ear not hear?
    Does he who formed the eye not see?
¹⁰Does he who disciplines nations not punish?
    Does he who teaches mankind lack knowledge?
¹¹The Lord knows all human plans;
    he knows that they are futile.
¹²Blessed is the one you discipline, Lord,
    the one you teach from your law;
¹³you grant them relief from days of trouble,
    till a pit is dug for the wicked.
¹⁴For the Lord will not reject his people;
    he will never forsake his inheritance.
¹⁵Judgment will again be founded on righteousness,
    and all the upright in heart will follow it.

— TEN —

NABAL
BEAUTY AND THE BEAST (PT. 2)

The Background

The story of Nabal is told in 1 Samuel 25. He is also mentioned in 1 Samuel 27:3; 30:5; 2 Samuel 2:2; 3:3.

The Story

The name Nabal means, literally, fool; and although one must wonder what his parents were thinking, it would be difficult to find another man so aptly named. Nabal was as foolish, rude, and ugly as his wife, Abigail, was beautiful and intelligent.

Besides Abigail, the only thing Nabal had going for him was his wealth. A Calebite from Maon, he owned a thousand goats, three thousand sheep, and property in the Judean town of Carmel. Scholars surmise that, in an era of arranged marriages, Nabal's wealth would have been seen by Abigail's parents as qualification enough for her hand.

Nabal's shepherds were pasturing sheep in the wilderness of Paran, where David and his band of fugitives had relocated following the death of Samuel. When the time came for the shepherds to shear Nabal's sheep, David sent ten young men to Carmel with a request. David's emissaries brought greetings, wished Nabal good health, and reminded him that David had provided protection for the shepherds and flocks while they were in the area. They indicated that they would be grateful if Nabal would be inclined to share some of the blessings that their protection had provided.

Nabal responded by insulting David, comparing him to a runaway servant and questioning his lineage. He made it clear that he had no intention of giving David and his men anything but a hard time.

When David's men returned with the report, David angrily mustered his troops, instructing four hundred of them to arm themselves for battle and the remaining two hundred to stay with the supplies.

Meanwhile, one of the servants told Abigail how Nabal had insulted David's men, even though they had provided protection for Nabal's herds. Abigail quickly gathered enough provisions to feed an army, loaded the supplies on donkeys, and delivered them to David. Her timely intervention saved the day, not to mention the lives of Nabal and every male in his household.

When Abigail returned home, she found Nabal throwing a party fit for a king, oblivious to the consequences of his actions. In high spirits, like a fool in his folly, Nabal had gotten drunk, clueless of the danger that had been bearing down on him.

In the morning, once Nabal was sober enough to comprehend, Abigail told him what she had done—how she had intercepted David as he rushed toward Nabal with four hundred men, how the provisions she provided had placated him, and how he had returned to the wilderness.

Nabal, now stone sober, realized the full import of her words and just how narrowly he had escaped catastrophe. The shock of the thing gave him a heart attack, and ten days later his body grew as hard and cold as his heart. He died as he had lived, every bit the fool that his name proclaimed.

Leadership Lessons

35. Acknowledge, with gratitude and grace, the debt you owe another.

Sheep-shearing time was a season of great celebration. Festivities were in full swing when David reminded Nabal that his profit would not have been so great if his shepherds had not been protected by David's men. David hoped that since his men had performed a valuable service for Nabal—providing voluntary protection for Nabal's flocks in a time when Philistine raids were common—Nabal would see fit to reward them with some much-needed provisions as a token of appreciation. Nabal refused to share anything and, as a consequence, lost everything.

When it is within your means, share your blessings with those through whom God has provided those blessings. At the very least, express your gratitude when others provide you with assistance.

36. Hurt feelings never justify hurtful actions.

David's anger was understandable. Nabal's words had been abrasive and offensive. Though he had been disrespected, David's response was based on raw emotions rather than reasoned judgment. He would later reflect that vengeance and retribution rightfully belong only to God. As John Trapp notes, "Little is there lost by making God our umpire."[1]

David learned a valuable lesson: Never let raging emotions dictate regrettable responses. "Wait on the Lord" will become a recurring theme in David's psalms.[2]

37. Good leaders have the wisdom to change their course when it becomes apparent they are going in the wrong direction.

It is helpful to compare the attitudes of Nabal and David. When Abigail presented her case to David, his heart softened and he reversed his decision. David had the wisdom to recognize wise counsel in Abigail's appeal. He was on a wrong course, and Abigail, through her bold, quick, and wise request, stopped him from a terrible mistake. On the other hand, when Abigail told the news to Nabal, his heart hardened in a combination of fear, anger, and shock.

Honest and accurate self-appraisal may be the most difficult of a leader's tasks. To do it well, you must actively seek evidence that you are wrong, rather than compiling evidence that you are right.[3]

Leaders need a reverse gear and the willingness to use it when needed.

Questions for Leadership Development

1. How easy is it for you to change your mind when you are given information that reveals the course of action you have chosen may be in error?

2. Under what circumstances does your personal leadership tend to reflect Nabal's style and in what ways does it reflect Abigail's style?[4]

3. What other leadership lessons can be derived from the story of Nabal?

The Psalm

Psalm 14 is very similar to Psalm 53, both of which refer to the foolishness of evildoers.

Psalm 14

For the director of music. Of David.

¹The fool says in his heart,
    "There is no God."
 They are corrupt, their deeds are vile;
    there is no one who does good.
²The LORD looks down from heaven
    on all mankind
 to see if there are any who understand,
    any who seek God.
³All have turned away, all have become corrupt;
    there is no one who does good,
    not even one.
⁴Do all these evildoers know nothing?
 They devour my people as though eating bread;
    they never call on the LORD.
⁵But there they are, overwhelmed with dread,
    for God is present in the company of the righteous.
⁶You evildoers frustrate the plans of the poor,
    but the LORD is their refuge.
⁷Oh, that salvation for Israel would come out of Zion!
    When the LORD restores his people,
    let Jacob rejoice and Israel be glad!

— ELEVEN —

ABISHAI
WHO'S GOT YOUR BACK?

The Background

The story of Abishai is told in 1 Samuel 26; 2 Samuel 3:30; 10:10-14; 16:9-11; 18:2-12; 20:5-10; 21:15-17; 23:17-19; 1 Chronicles 11:15-20; 18:11-12. He is also mentioned in 2 Samuel 2:18-24; 19:21; 1 Chronicles 2:16; 19:11-15.

The Story

Abishai was David's nephew—the oldest son of David's sister Zeruiah, and brother of Joab and Asahel. Abishai was one of the bravest and most impulsive of David's mighty men. He was a daring warrior, effective commander, and utterly loyal to his uncle, David.

Abishai's first biblical appearance occurs during Saul's pursuit of David in the desert of Ziph. Accompanied by three thousand elite troops, Saul's objective was to kill David. When David's scouts discovered Saul's location, Abishai volunteered to accompany David into Saul's camp under cover of darkness. They found Saul asleep in the camp, with his spear stuck in the ground beside him and his soldiers and Abner asleep around him. Abishai wanted to pin Saul to the ground with the spear, but David would not allow him to harm the Lord's anointed. Instead, they took Saul's spear and water jug and left the camp. Once they crossed the valley and were safely on the opposite hilltop, David called out to

Abner and Saul and told them what he had done. Saul recognized David's voice, and after a touching interchange between the two David went his way and Saul returned home.

After the death of Saul, when David had been anointed king over the tribe of Judah, war broke out between the houses of Saul and David. Abner, who had commanded Saul's army, made Ish-Bosheth, son of Saul, king over all Israel. The two armies then entered into a fierce battle, and Abner and the Israelites were defeated by David's men. As the combat concluded, Abishai's brother, Asahel, began to chase Abner. Abner warned him twice to break off the pursuit, and when he would not, Abner killed Asahel with the butt of his spear.

Soon after, Abner determined to go over to David's side and met with David in Hebron to plan the transition of the kingdom to David. When Joab learned of Abner's presence, he arranged a meeting with Abner and ruthlessly murdered him in revenge for the death of his brother Asahel. While Abishai's involvement in the murder is not specified, the murder was laid at the feet of both Joab and Abishai.

When Joab went to battle against the Arameans and the Ammonites, Abishai was put in command of the portion of the army deployed against the Ammonites, while Joab led the troops deployed against the Arameans. Both the Arameans and the Ammonites were put to flight.

During Absalom's rebellion, David and his men encountered a man named Shimei as they fled Jerusalem. Shimei cursed David and threw dirt on him, infuriating Abishai, who sought permission to cut off Shimei's head. Again, as he had in the case of King Saul, David decreed mercy and advised that God would take care of the issue.

When David's troops went to battle against Absalom, David divided his troops with a third under the command of Joab, a third under Abishai, and a third under Ittai the Gittite. After the battle was won, when David and his men were returning to Jerusalem, they encountered Shimei once again. Though Shimei was penitent and remorseful, Abishai again suggested death for Shimei. David, for a second time, restrained him and recommended mercy for Shimei.

After Absalom's rebellion, David next had to deal with a troublemaker named Sheba who had begun a secessionist movement in northern Israel. Amasa was originally dispatched to muster the troops against Sheba, but when he was late returning with troops, Abishai was sent to put down the rebellion. He was given command of Joab's men, the Kerethites and Pelethites, and all the mighty warriors, and saw his mission successfully completed.

It was Abishai who rescued an aging David from Ishbi-Benob, when the Philistine giant threatened to kill the king. A weary David was no match for the giant, who was armed with a seven-and-a-half pound bronze spearhead and a new sword. But Abishai struck him down and killed him, saving David's life. It was at that point that David's men swore that the king would never again go into battle with them, "so that the lamp of Israel will not be extinguished" (2 Sam. 21:17).

Abishai was one of the Thirty mighty men who formed David's bodyguard. In time, Abishai became chief of the Three—a trio of daring warriors who achieved fame for their military success in the face of overwhelming odds. As commander of David's elite guard, Abishai became as famous as the Three, though he was not one of them. Abishai's fame was assured after he withstood three hundred men and killed them with his spear. On one occasion, he struck down eighteen thousand Edomites in the Valley of Salt and followed up the victory by establishing military outposts in Edom.

Leadership Lessons

38. Most leaders will have a few followers who want to go too far in their zeal.

Abishai's temperamental nature had to be kept in check. His tendency was to respond to challenges by becoming destructive.

Abishai's solution to most "people problems" was to put the people to death. This is rarely a viable option for leaders, even those in the military. Effective leaders will seek to soften the response of overzealous followers while channeling their ability and passion in the right direction. It is better to task people like Abishai with dealing with problem people like Sheba rather than with dealing with problem people like Shimei.

David never put down Abishai's eager loyalty. Instead, he patiently tried to harness Abishai's energy and direct his passion. This approach, while not completely successful, saved David's life on at least one occasion. The day he was threatened by the giant Ishbi-Benob, David was grateful for Abishai's zealous protection.

Abishai's best trait—his unswerving loyalty to David—ensured that he would follow David's requests. His reliable allegiance enabled him to be useful, and David wisely knew how to put Abishai's abilities to most effective use.

39. It is not enough for leaders to be strong and effective; leaders must also have self-control and wisdom.

We admire Abishai's qualities of courage and loyalty. But we also recognize his lack of self-control and wisdom in dealing with people. At least three times, Abishai would have unnecessarily killed for the king if David had not stopped him.

As leaders respond to difficult people, they have opportunity to model appropriate responses for those who would follow. It is as important to know when to show mercy and grace as it is to know when to use strength and force.

40. Leaders must be able to determine what risks are acceptable.

When Abishai rescued David from the giant, the danger was very real and the consequences were far-reaching. David's troops realized how close they had come to prematurely losing their king and made David swear that he would not go into battle anymore in person, lest "the light of Israel" be prematurely extinguished.

Leaders need to be able to determine which risks are acceptable and which are unacceptable. Sometimes experience, training, or an innate sense will provide the right answer. Other times, the wise counsel of trusted advisers will be most valuable in determining appropriate risk.

Questions for Leadership Development

1. How do you help followers like Abishai, who sometimes act rashly and impulsively?

2. As a leader, how do you know which risks are acceptable and which are unacceptable?

3. How is loyalty different from friendship and kinship?

4. What other leadership lessons can be derived from the story of Abishai?

The Psalm

In Psalm 18, David remembers the deliverance he experienced in times of grave danger. The psalm recalls times when David was rescued from a "powerful enemy" and gives thanks to God for keeping David's "lamp burning."

Psalm 18:1-29

For the director of music. Of David the servant of the LORD. He sang to the LORD the words of this song when the LORD delivered him from the hand of all his enemies and from the hand of Saul. He said:

¹I love you, LORD, my strength.
²The LORD is my rock, my fortress and my deliverer;
　　my God is my rock, in whom I take refuge,
　　my shield and the horn of my salvation, my stronghold.
³I called to the LORD, who is worthy of praise,
　　and I have been saved from my enemies.
⁴The cords of death entangled me;
　　the torrents of destruction overwhelmed me.
⁵The cords of the grave coiled around me;
　　the snares of death confronted me.
⁶In my distress I called to the LORD;
　　I cried to my God for help.
　From his temple he heard my voice;
　　my cry came before him, into his ears.
⁷The earth trembled and quaked,
　　and the foundations of the mountains shook;
　　they trembled because he was angry.
⁸Smoke rose from his nostrils;
　　consuming fire came from his mouth,
　　burning coals blazed out of it.
⁹He parted the heavens and came down;
　　dark clouds were under his feet.
¹⁰He mounted the cherubim and flew;
　　he soared on the wings of the wind.

¹¹He made darkness his covering, his canopy around him—
  the dark rain clouds of the sky.
¹²Out of the brightness of his presence clouds advanced,
  with hailstones and bolts of lightning.
¹³The LORD thundered from heaven;
  the voice of the Most High resounded.
¹⁴He shot his arrows and scattered the enemy,
  with great bolts of lightning he routed them.
¹⁵The valleys of the sea were exposed
  and the foundations of the earth laid bare
 at your rebuke, LORD,
  at the blast of breath from your nostrils.
¹⁶He reached down from on high and took hold of me;
  he drew me out of deep waters.
¹⁷He rescued me from my powerful enemy,
  from my foes, who were too strong for me.
¹⁸They confronted me in the day of my disaster,
  but the LORD was my support.
¹⁹He brought me out into a spacious place;
  he rescued me because he delighted in me.
²⁰The LORD has dealt with me according to my righteousness;
  according to the cleanness of my hands he has rewarded me.
²¹For I have kept the ways of the LORD;
  I am not guilty of turning from my God.
²²All his laws are before me;
  I have not turned away from his decrees.
²³I have been blameless before him
  and have kept myself from sin.
²⁴The LORD has rewarded me according to my righteousness,
  according to the cleanness of my hands in his sight.
²⁵To the faithful you show yourself faithful,
  to the blameless you show yourself blameless,
²⁶to the pure you show yourself pure,
  but to the devious you show yourself shrewd.
²⁷You save the humble

but bring low those whose eyes are haughty.
[28]You, LORD, keep my lamp burning;
    my God turns my darkness into light.
[29]With your help I can advance against a troop;
    with my God I can scale a wall.

TWELVE

SAUL
WHEN A LEADER IMPLODES, OR DEATH BY AMALEKITE

The Background

The story of Saul is told in 1 Samuel 9—31; 2 Samuel 1—2; 21; 1 Chronicles 10:1-13. Other notable mentions include 2 Samuel 3:7-8, 13-14; 5:2; 7:15; 12:7; 22:1; 1 Chronicles 5:10; 8:1, 33; 9:35, 39; Psalms 18:1; 52:1; 54:1; 57:1; 59:1; Acts 13:21-22.

The Story

Saul, Israel's first king, was the son of Kish of the tribe of Benjamin and the father of Jonathan, Malki-Shua, Abinadab, and Ish-Bosheth. His daughters were Merab and Michal, and his wife was Ahinoam.

Saul's relationship with David can be divided into three distinct time periods: (1) Saul's coronation to the slaying of Goliath; (2) the slaying of Goliath to the exile of David; (3) the exile of David to the death of Saul.

Saul's Coronation to the Slaying of Goliath

Saul's rise to the kingship of Israel was unusual. Robert Pinsky notes, "Being king wasn't Saul's idea, it wasn't even exactly the idea of the sour prophet Samuel who anointed him. It was the people's idea."[1] Israel was clamoring for a king. All the surrounding nations had a king, and Israel wanted one too. Saul's introduction to the national stage occurred when some donkeys belonging to his father wandered away about the time God was telling Samuel to give in to Israel's wishes and anoint a king. Saul's father sent him in search for the donkeys at the same time God sent Samuel in search of Saul. It was a strange crossing of paths. When he found him, Samuel privately anointed Saul the first king of Israel.

God's choice of Saul remained a secret until Samuel made the announcement at Mizpah. When Samuel was ready to begin the press conference, Saul was nowhere to be seen. In an attempt to avoid the kingship, he was busy hiding in the luggage of the folks who had traveled to Mizpah. Tipped off to Saul's whereabouts by God himself, Samuel proceeded to flush him out of the luggage and into the light of day.[2]

After such a shaky inauguration, Saul's kingship begins impressively. A military crisis gave Saul opportunity to prove his leadership ability. The Ammonites had come to capture Jabesh Gilead, a border town on the far side of the Jordan, and the Ammonite king, Nahash, was promising to pluck out the right eye of every person in the town to humiliate them. Saul used the threat to forge a unified army out of the twelve scattered tribes. He cut a yoke of oxen into pieces and sent the parts to each of the tribes as an "unmistakable message of Saul's ruthless resolve, . . . *I will do anything I need to.*"[3] Having successfully mustered a national army, Saul proceeded to rescue the city of Jabesh from the Ammonites.

But then Saul makes three successive poor decisions. First, in 1 Samuel 13, Saul disregards Samuel's explicit instructions. Then, in 1 Samuel 14, Saul makes a rash vow that has serious consequences for his own son. Finally, in 1 Samuel 15, he blatantly disobeys God in the matter of the Amalekites. Saul's relationship with Samuel was strained from the beginning, but after Saul's sin in regard to the Amalekites, Samuel marches out to find Saul and tell him that he will no longer enjoy God's favor. After that, Samuel and Saul go their separate ways—Samuel to Ramah and Saul to Gibeah—never to meet again in life.

While God withdrew his blessing from Saul, he was not in a hurry to remove Saul from the kingship. At Gibeah, Saul began to slip into fits of depression over his abandonment by Samuel and God. The only cure for his fits of melancholy and madness was music, so the search was made for a musician who could calm Saul's foul moods. The services of a young shepherd named David were engaged, in hopes that David, skilled on the harp, might soothe the king. Saul was taken with David from the beginning, and David became not only the court musician called on to bring a measure of peace to Saul when tormented by an evil spirit but also his armor-bearer. From then on, whenever a tormenting spirit would come upon Saul, "David would take up his lyre and play. Then relief would come to Saul; he would feel better, and the evil spirit would leave him" (1 Sam. 16:23).

The Slaying of Goliath to the Exile of David

Apparently, David served as Saul's personal musician and shepherd of his own father's flocks at the same time. One morning David was performing an errand for his father—taking provisions to his three brothers serving in Saul's army—when he heard Goliath's daily defiance of God and Israel. Goliath's size and taunts had intimidated Saul's soldiers and broken their will to fight, just as Goliath intended. Even Saul was frightened by the giant, and found himself unable to go out and face him, all the more since Samuel had already told him that God was not on his side anymore. The reward Saul offered to whoever defeated the giant was riches, a royal princess, and tax relief.

David volunteered to battle the giant. The troops immediately escorted David to King Saul, who took one look at David and insisted that David wear the king's own armor. The problem was David wore a thirty-eight short and Saul wore a forty-six long. David insisted on fighting Goliath armed only with the weapons of a shepherd—a sling and a staff.

When David returned to Saul's tent carrying the head of Goliath, Saul realized there was a new hero in Israel. The people liked

David. They really liked David. This fact was not missed by Saul. Saul was still given to bouts of depression, and when that happened, the only person who could bring him out of it was David. But the king felt threatened by David, as leaders sometimes do when there is a popular, promising up-and-comer around. Saul also knew, as did David, that this shepherd/musician/boy-warrior just might have his job someday. The king became hardened with madness and jealousy. "Saul has slain his thousands, and David his tens of thousands" (1 Sam. 18:7), the people would sing. Saul began to smolder as he grew paranoid in his certainty that David was after his throne.

Saul devoted much time and energy in unsuccessful attempts to eliminate David. When his daughter, Michal, fell in love with David, Saul named a dowry that was intended to result in David's death at the hand of a hundred Philistines who would take exception to David's attempt to separate them from their foreskins. When that did not work, he made David captain of a thousand men and sent him off to fight the Philistines, hoping that the Philistines would kill David. David's victories only made Saul more sullen and desirous of David's death.

When it became obvious that David had won not only the love of Saul's daughter Michal but also the deep friendship of his son, Jonathan, Saul's intention to kill David only intensified.

Saul then sent a band of assassins to find David at Naioth. To Saul's dismay, the death squad became a church choir—prophesying in ecstasy. Two additional death squads resulted in a similar outcome. Finally, Saul himself went in search of David and fell under the same spiritual influence that had rendered his soldiers useless.

One day Saul took up a new tack. He threw a spear at David, trying to skewer him. Fortunately for David—and later for Jonathan—Saul was not accomplished at this warrior art. (He was 0-3 in the Bible.) On two separate occasions, Saul tried to shish-ke-bab David. David did not throw Saul's spears back at him. All he did was dodge the javelins when the king decided to use him for target practice.

The night Saul tried to kill him in his bed was the night David left for good. Saul sent a death squad to David's home to kill him.[4] Fortunately, they were intercepted and misled by Michal while David slipped away for what would become a very long season of exile.

The Exile of David to the Death of Saul

David fled without speaking a word or lifting a hand against Saul, and Saul began to hunt David. Saul became the hound and David the hare, put to flight and looking for a hole in which to hide. Others also suffered from the consequences of Saul's paranoia, including the entire population of Nob, murdered because one priest from the city innocently rendered aid to David.

Twice, while Saul was actively seeking to take David's life, David spared Saul's life. Early in the hunt, Saul was summoned home when word of a Philistine raid reached him, but he soon picked up David's trail again. At En Gedi, Saul went into a cave to relieve himself, unaware that David and his men were in the same cave, watching him. David's men encouraged him to kill Saul then and there, but David would not. He did, however, stealthily cut a piece from Saul's robe. When Saul left the cave, David walked out and made himself known, showing the piece cut from the king's clothing. Saul immediately recognized how close to death he had come and how David had spared him. Chagrined, he called off the hunt and returned home. "But the cycle keeps recurring, suspicion and forbearance and murderous intent, lurching on the contorted axle of Saul's brooding, his terrified rage at the quicksilver, evasive and invincible David," observes Pinsky.[5]

Driven by jealousy, hatred, and fear, Saul hunted David from the caves of Adullam, to the town of Keilah, to the En Gedi wilderness. David spent years on the run, with a death warrant on his head, and the player of songs became the writer of songs. In those caves David became the greatest hymn writer the world had ever known. Finally, David finds sanctuary with Achish and sets up camp in Ziklag, as Saul prepares to once again battle the Philistines.

On the eve of what would be his final battle, Saul, disguised as a commoner, sought out a medium under cover of darkness. He was undone by the encounter with the witch of Endor, who eerily managed to call up Samuel from the dead. Samuel, not happy to be bothered, predicted the imminent death of both Saul and his sons at the hands of the Philistines.

The next day Saul and his sons died on Mount Gilboa. Saul was mortally wounded by Philistine archers and either fell on his own sword or was put out of his misery by an Amalekite. When the Philistines came to "strip the slain" the next day, they desecrated the bodies of Saul and his sons by cutting off Saul's head and hanging his corpse and those of his sons on the city wall of Beth Shan.

Ironically, it was an Amalekite who brought the news of Saul's death to David.[6] The Amalekite claimed that he had administered the coup de grace on the dying king and had retrieved Saul's crown and band, which he presented to David. If the Amalekite thought he would be rewarded for this deed, he badly misjudged David, who immediately gave instructions that the Amalekite be executed for his impertinent brazenness.

The death of Jonathan and Saul moved David to eloquence.[7] It also moved the inhabitants of Jabesh Gilead to a heroic act of loyalty and devotion. The men of Jabesh Gilead, in tribute for Saul's deliverance of their city when he first became king, bravely recovered the bodies of Saul and his sons and gave them an honorable burial.

Leadership Lessons

41. Jealousy will destroy your effectiveness as a leader.

Saul had the appearance of a leader and was voted "most likely to succeed" by his senior class. If you were going to elect a king, Saul was a no-brainer. A head taller than anyone else in Israel, Saul had a commanding presence. But when the boyishly good-looking, musically gifted giant killer came along, Saul no longer saw the gifts and opportunities God had given him. Saul jealously saw only the gifts and opportunities God had given David. He saw in David a threat larger than Goliath. He saw in David a threat to his power and his position.

Saul became a suspicious, bitter, angry man. He was Israel's first king, and his accomplishments over his twenty-year reign are significant. Yet, he is remembered mostly for his madness. He was eaten up with jealousy, capable of murder, and willing to live in spiritual darkness.

Jealousy is a character flaw that will rob you of objectivity, make others unwilling to follow you or trust you, and render your leadership ineffective. Jealousy causes leaders to react with suspicion rather than wisdom. It distracts leaders from the true mission of the organization, leading them down rabbit trails of self-preservation and self-aggrandizement. Jealousy will cause a leader to implode, destroying from the inside.

You will not win the comparison game, so do not play it. If you fall short in your comparison with another, it leads to envy. If you come out ahead in your comparison to another, it leads to pride.

Great leaders attract great leaders. The better your leadership skills, the more likely other significantly gifted leaders will be on your team. If jealousy is an issue with you, be prepared to lose the best and brightest on your team.

42. In leadership, how you finish is more important than how you start.

Saul began his reign by seeking the guidance of God but ended his reign seeking the guidance of a witch. Saul began his reign by calling the nation to worship but ended his reign far from God. Saul began his reign with a great victory over the Ammonites but ended his reign with a great defeat at the hands of the Philistines.

It is important for leaders to start well. A good start instills confidence and credibility and allows for the development of momentum. But it is even more important for leaders to finish well.

A strong finish ensures legacy and allows a leader's example to provide a model of continued encouragement and lasting value to the organization.

43. You do not have to be the first one to throw the spear to be a spear thrower.

Saul was a spear thrower. When he felt threatened and in danger of losing power, he sought to eliminate the threat—be the threat real or imagined. Saul threw spears.

When Saul tried to kill David with the spear—and missed—David did not pick up the spear and throw it back. David did not throw spears. David could have divided the kingdom and overthrown Saul. Rather than do that, he packed up and left the kingdom. He fled rather than cause division.

You may be the kind of leader who is never the first to throw a spear. But if you are willing to throw a spear back, you are still a spear thrower. And you are a leader after the order of Saul.[8]

44. It is foolish to not eliminate Amalekites.

The dividing line between Saul's early successes and his later failures was his sin in the matter of the Amalekites. God had given specific instructions: completely destroy the Amalekites. Saul disobeyed the command—reserving the best of the people and the best of their possessions. Frederick Buechner suggests that of all the things Saul had going against him, the worst was himself.[9] The only person responsible for Saul's disobedience in the matter of the Amalekites was Saul himself.

If God tells you to get rid of the Amalekites, get rid of the Amalekites. Your disobedience will cost you, and it will cost you far more than you may realize. Saul's disobedience cost him Samuel's confidence, it cost him God's blessing, and it cost him his own health and well-being. Saul had been commanded to eliminate the Amalekites—a command he disregarded. The irony is that, in the end, it was an Amalekite that eliminated Saul.

Saul himself said, "I have played the fool."[10] Saul's self-description has been repeated by many leaders who have chosen spiritual disobedience rather than faithfulness to the Lord.

45. Speak well of your predecessor.

If anyone had reason to bad-mouth Saul, it was David. And yet, in all the chapters that tell the story of Saul and David, not once does David speak ill of Saul. In fact, the eulogy that David delivers at Saul's funeral is beautiful.[11] David exhibits a spirit of forgiveness and is magnanimous in his praise. His words honor the best of Saul's leadership and avoid any criticism of Saul's failures. No doubt, the men and women of Israel took note and appreciated David's generous spirit.

So much of what is negatively said about former leaders, and especially about our own predecessors, does not need to be said, either publicly or privately. Often, it reflects that we do not yet understand the factors that drove our predecessors to take the actions they did. One's criticism of one's predecessor does not make one stand any taller in the eyes of others, just as one's praise of one's predecessor does not make one stand any smaller in the eyes of others.

46. Leaders usually either become better or they become bitter.

The events of life will harden you or will break you. Life will make you better or bitter. The events of life have the ability to reveal the hidden motives of your own heart. David experienced brokenness. And in his brokenness, he allowed God to create the greatest king Israel ever had. Saul also experienced brokenness. And in his brokenness, he became hardened and bitter and unusable by God. Both Saul and David were anointed. The difference was their character.

Whether life makes you better or bitter will depend on whether you are a person after God's own heart or whether you are a leader who craves power and authority and desires that your own will be done.

It is not what happens to us in life that makes the difference. It is our response to what happens to us in life that makes the difference.

47. Leaders attract followers like themselves.

Saul had no giant killers in his army—except David—and David was soon chased off into exile by Saul. But 2 Samuel 21 contains the story of Abishai, a follower of David, who is also a giant killer. David seems to have attracted and embraced giant killers, while Saul was threatened and intimidated by giant killers.

Leaders tend to attract followers like them.

Questions for Leadership Development

1. What kind of a leader will you be—a leader after the order of Saul or a leader after the order of David?

2. How do you normally react when someone throws a spear at you?

3. Are you a leader who is growing better or growing bitter?

4. What other leadership lessons can be derived from the story of Saul?

The Psalm

Many of David's psalms were written while he was on the run from Saul. It was a season of brokenness for David, and he pours out his heart, his prayers, and his hopes in these spiritual songs. Psalm 57 is one such example.

Psalm 57

For the director of music. To the tune of "Do Not Destroy." Of David. A miktam. *When he had fled from Saul into the cave.*

¹Have mercy on me, my God, have mercy on me,
    for in you I take refuge.
I will take refuge in the shadow of your wings
    until the disaster has passed.
²I cry out to God Most High,
    to God, who vindicates me.
³He sends from heaven and saves me,
    rebuking those who hotly pursue me—
    God sends forth his love and his faithfulness.
⁴I am in the midst of lions;
    I am forced to dwell among ravenous beasts—
men whose teeth are spears and arrows,
    whose tongues are sharp swords.
⁵Be exalted, O God, above the heavens;
    let your glory be over all the earth.
⁶They spread a net for my feet—
    I was bowed down in distress.
They dug a pit in my path—
    but they have fallen into it themselves.
⁷My heart, O God, is steadfast,
    my heart is steadfast;
    I will sing and make music.
⁸Awake, my soul!
    Awake, harp and lyre!
    I will awaken the dawn.

[9]I will praise you, Lord, among the nations;
    I will sing of you among the peoples.
[10]For great is your love, reaching to the heavens;
    your faithfulness reaches to the skies.
[11]Be exalted, O God, above the heavens;
    let your glory be over all the earth.

— THIRTEEN —

AHINOAM
FOR BETTER, FOR WORSE

The Background

The story of Ahinoam is told in 1 Samuel 25:43; 27:3; 30:5; 2 Samuel 2:2; 3:2; 1 Chronicles 3:1.

The Story

Ahinoam was David's second wife. David married her after Michal—daughter of Saul and David's first wife—was given by Saul to Paltiel during David's exile. Very little is known about Ahinoam.[1] She was from Jezreel and David married her while he was on the run from King Saul in the wilderness of Paran. While David's marriage to Abigail is mentioned first, it is followed by the statement that he had previously married Ahinoam.

Soon after Achish gave the city of Ziklag to David as a place to live, David, his men, and all their families settled there and began using the town as a base of operations. From Ziklag, David would raid the nearby Amalekite villages, killing every man, woman, and child, and leaving utter destruction in his wake. This caused no small amount of bitterness; and so, when David and his men went to join the Philistines, leaving their homes and families unprotected, the Amalekites saw an opportunity to have their revenge. They descended on the village, plundering and burning all they could, kidnapping Ahinoam, along with Abigail and all the other people left behind in the city. When David and his men returned to Ziklag, they were devastated by the destruction they found.

Numb with horror and shock, David and his men gazed upon the blackened and smoldering ruins. As a sense of their terrible desolation burst upon them, those battle-scarred warriors "wept aloud until they had no strength left to weep" (1 Sam. 30:4). Not only did David have to deal with his own personal loss, but he also had to deal with the combined losses of his men, who, looking for someone to blame, had begun to talk about stoning him.

After consulting the ephod and gaining direction from God, David was able to rally his men. He began pursuit of the Amalekites with six hundred men, all of whom had been on the march the last three days. By the time they reached the brook at Besor, two hundred men had reached the point of exhaustion. David had those two hundred men stay at Besor and guard the supplies. Though his force was depleted by one-third, David and the four hundred continued on, found the Amalekites, attacked them, defeated them, killed all except four hundred who escaped on camels, and accomplished the safe return of all who had been taken hostage. From the Amalekites David also acquired plunder, which he sent to those he hoped would become his political allies throughout Judah. The gifts were sent to the leaders of the following towns where David and his men had been: Bethel, South Ramoth, Jattir, Aroer, Siphmoth, Eshtemoa, Rakal, Hormah, Bor Ashan, Athak, and Hebron and the towns of the Jerahmeelites and Kenites. Three days later David's exile ended with the news that Saul had been slain by the Philistines.

When David went up to Hebron to be anointed king of the tribe of Judah, Ahinoam and Abigail accompanied him. While in Hebron, David's firstborn son, Amnon, was born of Ahinoam. Ahinoam is not mentioned again after the birth of Amnon.

Leadership Lessons

48. The hardships faced by leaders are usually matched, and often exceeded, by the hardships faced by their families.

Being the spouse of a leader is not always glorious. Being married to someone on the run from the current king means a lot of traveling, danger, and very little security. Ahinoam may have attracted a man who would be king, but her life was marred by hardship and tragedy. Soon after her marriage she had to share her husband with David's third wife, she was taken captive by fierce raiders, and her only son was murdered by his half-brother.

Leaders should be aware of the struggles and sacrifices their spouses endure and appreciative of the support their spouses provide.

49. On the worst day of your life, it makes sense to turn to God.

The day David approached Ziklag and found the city on fire, his possessions stolen, and his family taken captive must have been the worst day of his life up to that point. Saul was trying to kill him, he was hiding out in the enemy's backyard, his home had been burned, his possessions taken, his family taken captive, and his team wanted to stone him.

What do you do when you experience overwhelming loss? The first thing David and his men did was weep. Tears are not a sign of weakness; they are a sign of grief. Leaders should recognize—concerning both themselves and their followers—that a sense of loss is naturally accompanied by mourning. There are many kinds of loss in life—financial, vocational, marital (divorce), physical (sickness, death). While grief may manifest itself in various ways, it is important to recognize that the origin of grief is the sense of loss.

Next, "David inquired of the LORD" (1 Sam. 30:8). When David sought wisdom and direction from God, he found the help he needed to win back what was lost, and more. Every family member who had been taken prisoner was returned. David recovered everything the Amalekites had taken away as well as everything else they had gained in their raids.

Leaders are wise to seek divine help, guidance, and encouragement for every challenge, especially those challenges that involve overwhelming loss.

50. When the Lord blesses you, consider blessing others.

When David defeated the Amalekites, he did not keep all the wealth he gained from them for himself. He shared the wealth with others. First, he shared the wealth with the four hundred men who were directly involved in the battle. Next, when David shared the blessings with the two hundred who guarded the supplies at Besor, some of the four hundred complained, saying, "They didn't come and fight with us, so why should they get any of the plunder? Give them what was stolen from them, but the rest is ours!" David responded, "We're not doing that. We're not going to be selfish with what the Lord has given us. He has kept us safe and led us to victory. We're on the same team. Some fight in battle, and some guard the supplies."[2] David's decision became policy for Israel.

Finally, when David arrived back in Ziklag, he gave some of the belongings he recovered to the elders of Judah and to his friends, telling them, "Here is a gift for you from the plunder of the Lord's enemies" (1 Sam. 30:26). The gifts were sent to the leaders of the towns in Judah with whom David wanted to build alliances. A few days later those same leaders would anoint David as king of Judah.

Questions for Leadership Development

1. What hardships, if any, has your family endured as a result of your leadership opportunities?

2. When facing a challenge, at what point do you turn to God for help?

3. What have you lost, especially in the area of relationships, which needs to be reclaimed?

4. What other leadership lessons can be derived from the story of Ahinoam?

The Psalm

As David stood among the smoldering ruins of Ziklag, the words of Psalm 18 may have been part of the prayer he offered as he sought God's guidance and as he affirmed that he would place his trust in God to help him.

Psalm 18

For the director of music. Of David the servant of the Lord. *He sang to the* Lord *the words of this song when the* Lord *delivered him from the hand of all his enemies and from the hand of Saul. He said:*

[1] I love you, Lord, my strength.

[2] The Lord is my rock, my fortress and my deliverer;
    my God is my rock, in whom I take refuge,
    my shield and the horn of my salvation, my stronghold.

[3] I called to the Lord, who is worthy of praise,
    and I have been saved from my enemies.

[4] The cords of death entangled me;
    the torrents of destruction overwhelmed me.

[5] The cords of the grave coiled around me;
    the snares of death confronted me.

[6] In my distress I called to the Lord;
    I cried to my God for help.
From his temple he heard my voice;
    my cry came before him, into his ears.

[7] The earth trembled and quaked,
    and the foundations of the mountains shook;
    they trembled because he was angry.

[8] Smoke rose from his nostrils;
    consuming fire came from his mouth,
    burning coals blazed out of it.

[9] He parted the heavens and came down;
    dark clouds were under his feet.

[10] He mounted the cherubim and flew;
    he soared on the wings of the wind.

¹¹He made darkness his covering, his canopy around him—
  the dark rain clouds of the sky.
¹²Out of the brightness of his presence clouds advanced,
  with hailstones and bolts of lightning.
¹³The LORD thundered from heaven;
  the voice of the Most High resounded.
¹⁴He shot his arrows and scattered the enemy,
  with great bolts of lightning he routed them.
¹⁵The valleys of the sea were exposed
  and the foundations of the earth laid bare
 at your rebuke, LORD,
  at the blast of breath from your nostrils.
¹⁶He reached down from on high and took hold of me;
  he drew me out of deep waters.
¹⁷He rescued me from my powerful enemy,
  from my foes, who were too strong for me.
¹⁸They confronted me in the day of my disaster,
  but the LORD was my support.
¹⁹He brought me out into a spacious place;
  he rescued me because he delighted in me.
²⁰The LORD has dealt with me according to my righteousness;
  according to the cleanness of my hands he has rewarded me.
²¹For I have kept the ways of the LORD;
  I am not guilty of turning from my God.
²²All his laws are before me;
  I have not turned away from his decrees.
²³I have been blameless before him
  and have kept myself from sin.
²⁴The LORD has rewarded me according to my righteousness,
  according to the cleanness of my hands in his sight.
²⁵To the faithful you show yourself faithful,
  to the blameless you show yourself blameless,
²⁶to the pure you show yourself pure,
  but to the devious you show yourself shrewd.
²⁷You save the humble

but bring low those whose eyes are haughty.
[28]You, LORD, keep my lamp burning;
my God turns my darkness into light.
[29]With your help I can advance against a troop;
with my God I can scale a wall.
[30]As for God, his way is perfect:
The LORD's word is flawless;
he shields all who take refuge in him.
[31]For who is God besides the LORD?
And who is the Rock except our God?
[32]It is God who arms me with strength
and keeps my way secure.
[33]He makes my feet like the feet of a deer;
he causes me to stand on the heights.
[34]He trains my hands for battle;
my arms can bend a bow of bronze.
[35]You make your saving help my shield,
and your right hand sustains me;
your help has made me great.
[36]You provide a broad path for my feet,
so that my ankles do not give way.
[37]I pursued my enemies and overtook them;
I did not turn back till they were destroyed.
[38]I crushed them so that they could not rise;
they fell beneath my feet.
[39]You armed me with strength for battle;
you humbled my adversaries before me.
[40]You made my enemies turn their backs in flight,
and I destroyed my foes.
[41]They cried for help, but there was no one to save them—
to the LORD, but he did not answer.
[42]I beat them as fine as windblown dust;
I trampled them like mud in the streets.
[43]You have delivered me from the attacks of the people;
you have made me the head of nations.

People I did not know now serve me,
⁴⁴   foreigners cower before me;

as soon as they hear of me, they obey me.
⁴⁵They all lose heart;

they come trembling from their strongholds.
⁴⁶The L<small>ORD</small> lives! Praise be to my Rock!

Exalted be God my Savior!
⁴⁷He is the God who avenges me,

who subdues nations under me,
⁴⁸   who saves me from my enemies.

You exalted me above my foes;

from a violent man you rescued me.
⁴⁹Therefore I will praise you, L<small>ORD</small>, among the nations;

I will sing the praises of your name.
⁵⁰He gives his king great victories;

he shows unfailing love to his anointed,

to David and to his descendants forever.

FOURTEEN

ABNER

AN ENEMY BECOMES AN ALLY

The Background

The story of Abner is told in 1 Samuel 14:50-51; 17:55-58; 26:5-14; 2 Samuel 2 and 3. He is also mentioned in 1 Samuel 20:25; 2 Samuel 4:1, 12; 1 Kings 2:5, 32; 1 Chronicles 26:28; 27:21.

The Story

Abner, commander of Saul's army, was Saul's cousin. He was the son of Ner, who was the brother of Kish, the father of King Saul.

As David was going out to meet Goliath, Saul tasked Abner with learning the identity of David's father. When David returned from killing Goliath, it was Abner who brought David to Saul, with David still holding the Philistine's head.

Abner was never far from Saul. He sat next to Saul at the king's table and slept near the king when the army was on maneuvers. Abner accompanied Saul when he was in pursuit of David. At one point Saul, accompanied by three thousand elite troops, was searching for David in the desert of Ziph. David, learning of Saul's location, was joined by Abishai on a covert nighttime mission into Saul's camp where they stealthily removed Saul's spear and water jug. As commander of the army, Abner was responsible for the king's safety. David took note of this and rebuked Abner by calling out to him from a safe distance and asking him why he had not been more diligent in protecting King Saul.

After Saul was killed in battle with the Philistines, Abner sought to see the kingship continue in Saul's line. He had Ish-Bosheth, Saul's forty-year-old son, made king of the northern tribes and all of Israel.

At the pool of Gibeon, Abner, leading Ish-Bosheth's army, and Joab, leading David's men, each chose twelve young men from their respective armies to engage in hand-to-hand combat. All twenty-four were killed when each fighter thrust a dagger into his opponent in what Pinsky calls the "impossibly symmetrical choreography of this mutual slaughter."[1] There followed a fierce, full-scale battle between the two armies, and Abner and the Israelites were defeated by David's men, losing 360 Benjamites to David's nineteen casualties. During the retreat from the battle, the real drama took place as Abner was pursued by Joab's fast-running brother, Asahel. Twice, Abner warned Asahel to turn aside, but Asahel refused. The experienced Abner executed a fatal move. Abner stopped suddenly and braced himself, while Asahel ran into the blunt end of Abner's spear, which pierced him under the fifth rib and exited his back. Though the deed was a legitimate combat action, Joab would nurse his hatred of Abner until he had opportunity for revenge. So began the blood feud between Abner and Joab.

As war between the house of Saul and the house of David wore on, Abner strengthened his position within the house of Saul. When Ish-Bosheth, who had succeeded Saul as king, accused Abner of sleeping with Saul's concubine, Rizpah, Abner was infuriated by the rebuke and immediately opened negotiations with David, promising to bring all Israel with him. He hoped that in exchange for his delivering Saul's kingdom, David would make him commander of his army. David made one condition for their meeting—that his wife, Michal, the daughter of Saul, should accompany Abner and be returned to David. Abner forced Ish-Bosheth, Michal's brother, to agree to the demand. When her husband, Paltiel, followed behind Michal weeping all the way, Abner ordered him to return home alone. Next, Abner consulted with the elders of Israel and encouraged them to make David their king. He then proceeded to Hebron to meet with David about the unification of the kingdom.

Despite Abner's former hostility, he and his twenty men were warmly and hospitably received by David. Just as Abner was leaving to assemble Israel for a covenant-making ceremony with David, Joab returned from a successful raid. He was incensed upon learning of David's meeting with Abner and attributed Abner's presence to treachery. It is hard to tell if Joab's motivation was vengeance or jealousy—whether he desired to avenge the death of his brother, Abishai, protect his position as general of David's army against a potential new rival, Abner, or maybe accomplish both goals at once.

As Abner was making his way from David's camp, Joab sent for him, without David's knowledge. When Abner returned, Joab led him into an inner room and murdered him by stabbing him in approximately the same place as Asahel's fatal wound.

To counter any backlash from this act, David reprimanded Joab publicly and proclaimed a season of mourning. The nation accepted David's innocence in the matter. While Joab and the people with him walked in mourning in front of Abner, David himself walked behind the bier and delivered the eulogy. David wept aloud as Abner was buried in Hebron and sang a lament he had penned for Abner. It is a lament for one betrayed rather than one fallen in battle:

"Should Abner have died as the lawless die?

Your hands were not bound,

your feet were not fettered.

You fell as one falls before the wicked." (2 Sam. 3:33–34)

Abner's death effectively brought an end to the civil war. When Ish-Bosheth heard of it, he lost courage, and all Israel became alarmed. Soon after, Ish-Bosheth was assassinated by Rekab and Baanah, and David became the only claimant to the throne still remaining.

Leadership Lessons

51. It is possible for opponents to become allies.

The honest compliments of an opponent are often the best measure of someone's greatness. Although Abner and David spent much of their lives on competing sides, the Bible gives a glimpse of the respect they had for each other. As a young man, David had served under Abner. But later, Saul's campaign to kill David was led by Abner. Long accustomed to viewing David through the eyes of Saul, after Saul's death Abner temporarily upheld the power of the king's family. Eventually the tension between Abner and Saul's heir, Ish-Bosheth, brought about Abner's decision to support David's claim to the throne.

David's goal was the unification of the kingdom, not victory in a civil war. He was open to Abner's overtures and negotiations. During his efforts to unite the kingdom, Abner was murdered by Joab. David's response at Abner's death is evidence that the relationship had been restored.

Treat your adversary with respect. Today's opponent may become tomorrow's ally.

52. Honorable leaders will not condone the dishonorable actions of their followers.

The behavior of some gives evidence that they will do whatever is necessary to advance their cause. Joab resorted to duplicity and murder to advance his cause. He claimed he was doing David a great service by eliminating Abner. In reality, Joab was doing himself a great service.

When Joab murdered Abner, David immediately stated his own innocence of Abner's blood and cursed Joab: "I and my kingdom are forever innocent before the LORD concerning the blood of Abner son of Ner. May his blood fall on the head of Joab and on his whole family! May Joab's family never be without someone who has a running sore or leprosy or who leans on a crutch or who falls by the sword or who lacks food" (2 Sam. 3:28–29). For one to have a running sore or be leprous was to be excluded from the community and worship. The curse had social, spiritual, and physical implications for Joab and his descendants.

David sought to do something extremely difficult in a time of civil war—heal a nation. Joab's act would have made that healing impossible if David had not been a man of character and humility. Again, David placed an extremely difficult situation in God's hands—"May the LORD repay the evildoer according to his evil deeds" (2 Sam. 3:39). Joab acted in hate to appease his desire for personal vengeance. David acted with respect in his desire to heal a nation.

Distance yourself from the immoral actions of followers.

53. Sometimes the real leader is not the one with the title.

In the case of Ish-Bosheth and Abner, there can be no doubt that the real leader was Abner, even though Ish-Bosheth was the king.

In any organization, the real leaders are the ones who have the ability to make decisions, the opportunity to determine direction, and the influence to see those decisions implemented, whether or not they have the titles.

Questions for Leadership Development

1. What are the pros and cons of an opponent becoming an ally?

2. How could you "bridge the gap" between yourself and an opponent?

3. Which would you prefer: a weak leader whom you could control or a strong leader whom you could trust? Why?

4. What other leadership lessons can be derived from the story of Abner?

The Psalm

In Psalm 26, David proclaims his trust in God and appeals to God for vindication for his innocence in the evildoing of others.

Psalm 26

Of David.
[1]Vindicate me, LORD,
    for I have led a blameless life;
 I have trusted in the LORD
    and have not faltered.
[2]Test me, LORD, and try me,
    examine my heart and my mind;
[3]for I have always been mindful of your unfailing love
    and have lived in reliance on your faithfulness.
[4]I do not sit with the deceitful,
    nor do I associate with hypocrites.
[5]I abhor the assembly of evildoers
    and refuse to sit with the wicked.
[6]I wash my hands in innocence,
    and go about your altar, LORD,
[7]proclaiming aloud your praise
    and telling of all your wonderful deeds.
[8]LORD, I love the house where you live,
    the place where your glory dwells.
[9]Do not take away my soul along with sinners,
    my life with those who are bloodthirsty,
[10]in whose hands are wicked schemes,
    whose right hands are full of bribes.
[11]I lead a blameless life;
    deliver me and be merciful to me.
[12]My feet stand on level ground;
    in the great congregation I will praise the LORD.

FIFTEEN

ISH-BOSHETH
A THRONE WITHOUT A SCEPTER

The Background

The story of Ish-Bosheth is told in 2 Samuel 2—4.

The Story

Little is known about Ish-Bosheth, the youngest of Saul's four sons, and the only one who survived him. Ish-Bosheth is conspicuously absent from the account when his father and his brothers died on Mount Gilboa. Nor is he mentioned when the men of Jabesh Gilead retrieve the bodies of Saul, Jonathan, Malki-Shua, and Abinadab from the city walls where the Philistines put them on display.

After the death of Saul, Abner had the military and political muscle to arrange for the transfer of power to the only remaining son of Saul. Abner took Ish-Bosheth to Mahanaim and had him proclaimed king over Gilead, Ashuri, Jezreel, Ephraim, Benjamin, and all Israel. The tribe of Judah, however, remained loyal to David.

Ish-Bosheth was forty years old and proved to be an ineffective leader. He would be king in name only for two years; Abner was the real power behind the throne.

Ish-Bosheth's troops, under the command of Abner, suffered a devastating defeat at the hands of Joab and David's troops at Gibeon. As the war between the house of David and the house of Saul wore on, Ish-Bosheth became weaker while David grew stronger. All the while Abner was strengthening his position in the house of Saul.

Things went from bad to worse when Ish-Bosheth accused Abner of sleeping with Saul's concubine, Rizpah. The story does not reveal if Ish-Bosheth's suspicion was true, but Abner's alleged action would have been interpreted as a clear play for the throne. Abner's denial was angry and quick. He proclaimed his loyalty—not to Ish-Bosheth—but to "the house of your father Saul and to his family and friends" (2 Sam. 3:8). Abner also reminded Ish-Bosheth that he had not been handed over to David, though Abner had the power to accomplish that very thing. Ish-Bosheth was intimidated by Abner's response and let the matter drop.

When David sent messengers demanding that Michal be returned to him, the threat of David's army was enough to make Ish-Bosheth comply with the request. He gave orders that Michal (Ish-Bosheth's sister) be taken away from her second husband, Paltiel, despite Paltiel's obvious distress.

When Abner was murdered by Joab, all Israel was shaken and Ish-Bosheth lost what courage he had. Not long after, Ish-Bosheth was assassinated while taking his customary midday nap. Two of Ish-Bosheth's own army captains, Rekab and Baanah, stabbed him in the stomach, hacked off his head, and made their escape. They made their way to Hebron with the king's head and presented it to David, expecting a reward. David ordered their immediate execution for murdering an innocent man in his own bed and had the head of Ish-Bosheth buried in Abner's tomb at Hebron.

Ish-Bosheth's death ended the dynasty of Saul.

Leadership Lessons

54. He who makes the decisions is the king.

Following the death of King Saul, Abner possessed the military and political power to arrange for Ish-Bosheth to be named king. Abner, the king-maker, took the lead and personally arranged for the transfer of power. But the man he made king was a weak leader. Even though Ish-Bosheth was king, Abner wielded the real power behind Ish-Bosheth's monarchy.

Weak leaders are often manipulated by strong followers, who are in reality the real leaders. This can happen in the boardroom as well as on the battlefield. If weak leaders are aware of their own lack of competence, it is possible for those shortcomings to be addressed through training and education. It is a different matter if the shortcoming is in the area of courage. Courage cannot be taught. It can, however, be discovered. Courage is seen when a leader's strength of character and conviction is equal to the challenge being faced.

55. Heredity is no guarantee that one will be a good leader.

Throughout history, leadership succession has often been determined by heredity. While genetics and certain environmental factors, like growing up in a palace, can be great blessings, they do not guarantee leadership qualities. Just because Ish-Bosheth's father was king did not automatically mean that Ish-Bosheth had the gift mix, skill set, or disposition to be an effective king.

As the son of King Saul, Ish-Bosheth would have been privy to many privileges. Ish-Bosheth may have had royal blood, but he did not have royal bearing. He did little to distinguish himself as a competent leader. There is much that suggests he was a puppet king.

Abner had the power and ability for leadership, but not the birthright of leadership. Ish-Bosheth had the birthright of leadership, but not the power or ability for leadership. The two needed each other. Once Abner was eliminated, Ish-Bosheth was doomed.

56. Patient waiting, rather than rash action, can position leaders for opportunity.

After a troubled and uncertain reign, Ish-Bosheth's death cleared the way for David to assume the throne of Judah and Israel. Kevin J. Mellish notes that by the end of 2 Samuel 4, "four important men associated with the house of Saul had been killed: Saul, Jonathan,

Abner, and Ish-Bosheth. With each of these men eliminated, the path to kingship opened wider and wider to David."[1]

David had done nothing to bring about the demise of any of the leaders associated with the house of Saul. In the case of Saul, Jonathan, and Abner, David steadfastly refused to bring harm to them, even when the opportunities presented themselves. David would not use immoral means to achieve the throne of Israel. As a result, when the right time came, it was easier to unify the nation because of David's innocence in the deaths of the leaders of the house of Saul.

Questions for Leadership Development

1. Under what circumstances is it appropriate to switch allegiance from one leader to another?

2. In what ways can both nature and nurture contribute to leadership potential?

3. What other leadership lessons can be derived from the story of Ish-Bosheth?

The Psalm

In Psalm 139, David proclaims the nearness of God and announces his desire that God would bring justice upon those who are bloodthirsty and evil in their ways.

Psalm 139

For the director of music. Of David. A psalm.

¹You have searched me, LORD,
　and you know me.
²You know when I sit and when I rise;
　you perceive my thoughts from afar.
³You discern my going out and my lying down;
　you are familiar with all my ways.
⁴Before a word is on my tongue
　you, LORD, know it completely.
⁵You hem me in behind and before,
　and you lay your hand upon me.
⁶Such knowledge is too wonderful for me,
　too lofty for me to attain.
⁷Where can I go from your Spirit?
　Where can I flee from your presence?
⁸If I go up to the heavens, you are there;
　if I make my bed in the depths, you are there.
⁹If I rise on the wings of the dawn,
　if I settle on the far side of the sea,
¹⁰even there your hand will guide me,
　your right hand will hold me fast.
¹¹If I say, "Surely the darkness will hide me
　and the light become night around me,"
¹²even the darkness will not be dark to you;
　the night will shine like the day,
　for darkness is as light to you.
¹³For you created my inmost being;
　you knit me together in my mother's womb.

¹⁴I praise you because I am fearfully and wonderfully made;
  your works are wonderful,
  I know that full well.
¹⁵My frame was not hidden from you
    when I was made in the secret place,
    when I was woven together in the depths of the earth.
¹⁶Your eyes saw my unformed body;
    all the days ordained for me were written in your book
    before one of them came to be.
¹⁷How precious to me are your thoughts, God!
    How vast is the sum of them!
¹⁸Were I to count them,
    they would outnumber the grains of sand—
    when I awake, I am still with you.
¹⁹If only you, God, would slay the wicked!
    Away from me, you who are bloodthirsty!
²⁰They speak of you with evil intent;
    your adversaries misuse your name.
²¹Do I not hate those who hate you, Lᴏʀᴅ,
    and abhor those who are in rebellion against you?
²²I have nothing but hatred for them;
    I count them my enemies.
²³Search me, God, and know my heart;
    test me and know my anxious thoughts.
²⁴See if there is any offensive way in me,
    and lead me in the way everlasting.

SIXTEEN

BAANAH AND REKAB
DUMB AND DUMBER

The Background
The story of Baanah and Rekab is told in 2 Samuel 4:2-9.

The Story
Baanah and Rekab[1] were brothers. Commanders of raiding bands in Ish-Bosheth's army, they were the brutal and miscalculating sons of Rimmon the Beerothite, a Benjamite.

After Abner's death, Baanah and Rekab realized Ish-Bosheth's governance was doomed and assassinated him one afternoon as he was taking a nap. They entered his palace under the pretext of getting supplies and stabbed him in the stomach while he was sleeping in his own bed. They then beheaded the king before making their escape.

The two brothers traveled through the night to offer the grisly present of Ish-Bosheth's head to David, thinking that he would reward them for their action. The reaction of the king was quite different than they had anticipated. A shocked David accused them of being wicked men who killed an innocent man while he was sleeping in his own bed and immediately issued their death sentence. Their hands and feet were cut off and their bodies were hung by the pool in Hebron, a reminder to all that such conduct would not be tolerated.

Leadership Lessons

57. Be careful what you bless.

Though it could be argued that David benefitted from the action of Baanah and Rekab, he was careful not to reward their brazen deed. Rather, he punished behavior that amounted to high treason and murder. David responded to the brothers in much the same way as he did to the Amalekite who brought news of the death of Saul. He even alluded to the fate of the Amalekite before sentencing Baanah and Rekab to a similar end.

Leaders must be careful what they bless. When immoral, illegal, or unethical activity is rewarded, it only promotes more of the same. Such activity should not be condoned.

58. The means are as important as the ends.

While the death of Ish-Bosheth proved helpful to David's cause, the means of Ish-Bosheth's demise was immoral. Baanah and Rekab may have thought they were hastening the inevitable transfer of the throne to David, but what their crime hastened was their own demise.

Even when the result of an action brings about positive benefits, those benefits can be reversed if the means used is inappropriate.

Questions for Leadership Development

1. Can you recall observing a situation where the positive results of an action were negated because the action was achieved through inappropriate means?

2. When have you been tempted to adopt an "ends justifies means" mentality?

3. What other leadership lessons can be derived from the story of Baanah and Rekab?

The Psalm

Psalm 9 proclaims thanksgiving to God for his power over his enemies and his avenging the blood of the innocent.

Psalm 9

For the director of music. To the tune of "The Death of the Son." A psalm of David.

¹I will give thanks to you, LORD, with all my heart;
    I will tell of all your wonderful deeds.
²I will be glad and rejoice in you;
    I will sing the praises of your name, O Most High.
³My enemies turn back;
    they stumble and perish before you.
⁴For you have upheld my right and my cause,
    sitting enthroned as the righteous judge.
⁵You have rebuked the nations and destroyed the wicked;
    you have blotted out their name for ever and ever.
⁶Endless ruin has overtaken my enemies,
    you have uprooted their cities;
    even the memory of them has perished.
⁷The LORD reigns forever;
    he has established his throne for judgment.
⁸He rules the world in righteousness
    and judges the peoples with equity.
⁹The LORD is a refuge for the oppressed,
    a stronghold in times of trouble.
¹⁰Those who know your name trust in you,
    for you, LORD, have never forsaken those who seek you.
¹¹Sing the praises of the LORD, enthroned in Zion;
    proclaim among the nations what he has done.
¹²For he who avenges blood remembers;
    he does not ignore the cries of the afflicted.
¹³LORD, see how my enemies persecute me!
    Have mercy and lift me up from the gates of death,

[14]that I may declare your praises
    in the gates of Daughter Zion,
    and there rejoice in your salvation.
[15]The nations have fallen into the pit they have dug;
    their feet are caught in the net they have hidden.
[16]The LORD is known by his acts of justice;
    the wicked are ensnared by the work of their hands.
[17]The wicked go down to the realm of the dead,
    all the nations that forget God.
[18]But God will never forget the needy;
    the hope of the afflicted will never perish.
[19]Arise, LORD, do not let mortals triumph;
    let the nations be judged in your presence.
[20]Strike them with terror, LORD;
    let the nations know they are only mortal.

SEVENTEEN

JOAB
THE MISTAKE OF OVERLOOKING CHARACTER

The Background

The story of Joab is told in 2 Samuel 2—3; 10—11; 12:26-27; 14; 18—20; 24:1-9; 1 Kings 1—2; 1 Chronicles 11:6-8; 19:8-19; 21:1-6. He is also mentioned in 1 Samuel 26:6; 2 Samuel 8:16; 2 Samuel 17:25; 23:18, 24, 37; 1 Kings 11:15, 16, 21; 1 Chronicles 2:16; 11:20, 26, 39; 18:15; 20:1; 26:28; 27:24, 34; Psalm 60:1.

The Story

Joab was David's nephew, the son of David's sister Zeruiah, and became commander of David's army as reward for capturing the Jebusite stronghold that became Jerusalem. Joab had two brothers, Abishai and Asahel. Like his brothers, Joab was an elite warrior, but was evidently the stronger leader and strategist, emerging as the leader of his brothers even before being made David's top commander. As general over David's armies, Joab led successful military campaigns against Syria, Ammon, Moab, and Edom. Following the death of Saul, war broke out between the house of David (Judah) and the house of Saul (Israel). Joab led David's men in a defeat of Abner and the army of Israel at the pool of Gibeon, killing 360 Benjamites while losing only nineteen men of Judah. When Abner and his men took flight, Joab's brother, Asahel, pursued Abner. Asahel ignored Abner's repeated warnings to turn aside, and Abner struck him down in self-defense.

When Joab learned that Abner had met with David to negotiate a unification of the kingdoms and transfer of his allegiance to David, Joab confronted David with suspicions of Abner's deceit and then quickly hatched a treacherous plan of his own. A messenger was sent to recall the unsuspecting Abner, and in revenge for Asahel's death Joab murdered Abner by stabbing him in the belly. David pronounced a curse upon Joab for the ruthless murder, but he did not dismiss him or punish him.[1]

After the civil war had settled down, war broke out against the Ammonites, and Joab led the army out to face them. The Israelites routed them, and they fled to safety within the walls of Rabbah[2] forcing Joab to lay siege to the city. It was during this campaign that Joab's complicity enabled David to eliminate Uriah after David made Uriah's wife, Bathsheba, pregnant. When Joab brought Rabbah to a point of capitulation by seizing its water supply, he sent for David, presenting him with the opportunity to take credit for the capture of the city.

Later, when Absalom had been banished for murdering Amnon, it was Joab who played an instrumental role in ending the estrangement between David and Absalom. He hatched a plot involving an actress from Tekoa, having her approach the king with a tale about her two sons, one of whom had been murdered by the other. The tribe wanted to execute her only remaining son, and she fell on her face before David, begging him to spare her only remaining heir. In response to her plea for mercy, David promised the remaining son would be spared. When the woman used his own words to challenge him to bring Absalom back, David recognized Joab's hand in the performance. Joab was instructed to bring Absalom back to Jerusalem, but Absalom was forbidden to see David.

Two years passed, during which Joab twice received messages from Absalom requesting an audience. When Joab ignored the requests, Absalom had his servants set Joab's barley field on fire, which quickly resulted in the desired meeting with Joab. Absalom pressed Joab to take his request to David. Joab relented, as did David, and Absalom was invited to an audience with the king.

All was not well, however, for in short time Absalom led a revolt and rallied most of Israel against his father, appointing Amasa to lead his army. In preparation for battle against Absalom, David divided his troops, with Joab, Abishai, and Ittai each given command of one-third of the forces. David gave specific instructions that Absalom was to be shown mercy.

During the battle, when Joab was told that Absalom had been caught by his hair in an oak tree, he first scolded the informer for not having killed Absalom, and then cold-bloodedly plunged three javelins into Absalom's heart while ten of Joab's armor-bearers finished Absalom off.

When David learned of Absalom's death, he was overwhelmed with grief. His deep mourning demoralized the army, who crept back into town with their heads down. Joab chastised the king with the news that the army was in danger of deserting him if he did not show his appreciation for their valor and victory. David went out and sat by the gate to pay tribute to the troops.

Following the death of Absalom, David decided to keep Amasa as commander of the army in place of Joab. When a troublemaker named Sheba began a secessionist movement, it was Amasa, not Joab, who was dispatched to Judah to muster the troops and put down the revolt. David gave Amasa three days to accomplish the task. When he had not returned as asked, David, believing time was of the essence, sent Abishai (Joab's brother) to put down Sheba's uprising, giving him command of Joab's men. As Amasa was returning to Jerusalem, he encountered the force deployed against Sheba. Joab, accompanying the army, pretended to kiss the unsuspecting Amasa, but instead murdered him by stabbing him in the belly. With Amasa eliminated, Joab assumed command of the army.

Meanwhile, Sheba had found sanctuary within the walls of the city of Abel. Joab placed the city under siege and began to knock down the city walls. A wise old woman from the city sought audience with Joab and asked why he was set on destroying an important city in Israel. Joab told her that he would withdraw from the city if Sheba were handed over. Sheba's head was soon thrown over the city wall. The army had left Jerusalem with Abishai in command; it returned to Jerusalem with Joab in command.

When David decided to take a census to determine the number of fighting men in Israel and Judah, Joab tried to talk him out of it, but was overruled.[3] Joab pressed the matter. David told him to stop being insubordinate. Joab found the task repulsive, and his count did not include all the tribes.

Toward the end of David's reign, Joab supported Adonijah's attempt to usurp the throne. David named Solomon as his successor and gave him instructions to take care of some unfinished business. David identified Joab as the murderer of Abner and Amasa and charged Solomon, "Do not let his gray head go down to the grave in peace" (1 Kings 2:6).

When Adonijah made a second attempt for the throne, Solomon took care of the unfinished business David had left him. Recalling that Adonijah had previously found mercy by fleeing to the tent of the Lord and clinging to the horns of the altar, Joab hurried to the altar in an effort to save himself. However, Solomon sent Benaiah[4] to execute Joab where he was, ensuring that his gray head did not go down to the grave in peace. Joab, who by some accounts had a distinguished career, was thus extinguished in shame.

Leadership Lessons

59. As leaders build their teams, they are wise to consider character to be more essential than competency.

David gave Joab a battlefield promotion to commander of the army on the basis of one accomplishment—the results produced in one battle—the capture of Jerusalem (1 Chron. 22:6). As far as we know, Joab's character and integrity were not considered in the appointment.

Before long Joab had not only shed enemy blood but also shed innocent blood. Ruthless and brutal, Joab was the kind of leader who reacts in jealous anger and leaves destruction in his wake. You can hardly find a failure among his military exploits, but he was prone to kill potential rivals as easily as real enemies.

During the assessment and evaluation of potential ministers, we often speak of "gifts and graces." Gifts refer to talents, abilities, and skills that are often most evident in public settings. Graces refer to the day-to-day ability of ministers to relate to people—even problem people—in ways that bless them rather than offending or alienating them. Individuals who have "gifts" but are lacking in "graces" often create more problems than they solve.

Be careful whom you put on your team. Choose poorly and you will be dealing with a burden rather than a blessing. You will spend significant time cleaning up the messes and rescuing those capsized in the wake of bad behavior. Character is as important as competency; integrity is as important as ability. Character matters in leadership.

60. Those who grow fond of power and position will be tempted to use unjust means to maintain power and position.

For many years David had to deal gingerly with the dangerous old general, Joab, and his bloody actions. This may have been due, in part, to Joab's knowledge of David's own character flaws, or it may have been due to David's fear of a strong man who holds on so tightly to his grudges. Maybe he simply tolerated Joab's flaws because of his military usefulness. No matter the reason, as time passed, it gradually became more and more difficult to remove Joab from his position of leadership. David attempted twice to remove Joab, only to see him eliminate his replacements. When Amasa threatened his position, Joab murdered him; when Abner became a rival for David's attention, Joab eliminated him. No one was going to take Joab's place.

Mohler cautions, "There is no escaping power, and there is no way to lead without it. The real issue is what kind of power a leader should possess and how that power is exercised."[5] Once persons attain positions of power, it is sometimes difficult to remove them; some will protect their position at any cost.

61. It is better to do nothing than to take action that will compromise your own integrity.

After Joab killed Abner, David acknowledged his own inability to control Joab, adding that Joab and Abishai were "too strong" for him (2 Sam. 3:39). Apparently, Joab was one problem that David could not solve. Outside of his outward mourning and expressions of anger, David did nothing. It may have been that David recognized that short of adopting Joab's tactics, he would be unable to remove him. There may be times when it appears that there is nothing we can do to positively affect a situation and maintain our integrity. What leaders must be careful not to do is sacrifice their own character by dealing with problem people in ways that are unethical and inappropriate. The ends do not justify the means. Better to do nothing than to adopt the methods of those who lack character and integrity.

The time will come when it is appropriate to take action. For David, the time came when Solomon succeeded him. The transition provided opportunity to take care of unfinished business. For those leaders caught in the middle of their own difficult and seemingly unsolvable problems, the time will also come to take action. Until that time, one will do well to remember the Serenity Prayer: "God grant me the serenity to accept the things I cannot change, the courage to change the things I can, and the wisdom to know the difference."

Questions for Leadership Development

1. What steps can you take to ensure that individuals you are considering adding to your team are persons of character and integrity?

2. In your leadership experience, how common is it for persons in positions of power and influence to be dominated by selfish ambition?

3. What do you do when a loose cannon is "too strong" for you?

4. What other leadership lessons can be derived from the story of Joab?

The Psalm

In Psalm 60, David testifies of his reliance upon and dependency upon God rather than people. The psalm was written on the occasion of one of Joab's greatest victories.

Psalm 60

For the director of music. To the tune of "The Lily of the Covenant." A miktam of David. For teaching. When he fought Aram Naharaim and Aram Zobah, and when Joab returned and struck down twelve thousand Edomites in the Valley of Salt.

¹You have rejected us, God, and burst upon us;
    you have been angry—now restore us!
²You have shaken the land and torn it open;
    mend its fractures, for it is quaking.
³You have shown your people desperate times;
    you have given us wine that makes us stagger.
⁴But for those who fear you, you have raised a banner
    to be unfurled against the bow.
⁵Save us and help us with your right hand,
    that those you love may be delivered.
⁶God has spoken from his sanctuary:
    "In triumph I will parcel out Shechem
    and measure off the Valley of Sukkoth.
⁷Gilead is mine, and Manasseh is mine;
    Ephraim is my helmet,
    Judah is my scepter.
⁸Moab is my washbasin,
    on Edom I toss my sandal;
    over Philistia I shout in triumph."
⁹Who will bring me to the fortified city?
    Who will lead me to Edom?
¹⁰Is it not you, God, you who have now rejected us
    and no longer go out with our armies?

[11]Give us aid against the enemy,
for human help is worthless.
[12]With God we will gain the victory,
and he will trample down our enemies.

EIGHTEEN

ABIATHAR
THE LOYALTY FACTOR

The Background

The story of Abiathar is told in 1 Samuel 22; 23:4-12; 30:7; 2 Samuel 15; 1 Kings 1; 2:22-35. He is also mentioned in 2 Samuel 8:17; 17:15; 19:11; 20:25; 1 Kings 4:4; 1 Chronicles 15:11; 18:16; 24:6; 27:34; and Mark 2:26.

The Story

When Saul had the priests of Nob massacred, there was only one survivor—Abiathar, the son of Ahimelek the high priest.[1] Abiathar fled to David with the news and when David invited him to stay and assured his safety, he joined David's band of men.

Abiathar brought the ephod with him when he came to David. The ephod was an article of clothing—a holy vest worn by the high priest. David believed it represented the divine presence and regularly used it to discern the will of the Lord. He consulted the ephod for direction about attacking the Philistines at Keilah, about whether to stay in Keilah when Saul was plotting against him, and about whether he should pursue the Amalekites who had raided Ziklag.

Apparently, Abiathar and Zadok shared the high priesthood between them during the reign of David. They, along with the Levites, brought the ark of the covenant to Jerusalem for the first time.

Abiathar was of great service to David, especially during Absalom's rebellion. As David fled Jerusalem at the onset of Absalom's revolt, Abiathar and Zadok removed the ark from the city, and Abiathar offered sacrifices as David's followers left the city. David then instructed Abiathar and Zadok, along with their sons, to return to Jerusalem with the ark and to provide information to David from that location. After Absalom's revolt was put down, Abiathar and Zadok helped pave the way with the elders of Judah for David to return to the palace as king.

Toward the end of David's reign, when it became apparent that a transition would soon take place, Abiathar made the unfortunate decision to support Adonijah when he set himself up as king. As a result, Solomon deprived Abiathar of the high priesthood and banished him to his estate at Anathoth, leaving Zadok to be the sole high priest. With this deposition, the rule of the house of Eli came to an end, as had been foretold 150 years before.[2]

Leadership Lessons

62. Wise leaders will seek wisdom and direction from God.

When David was faced with important decisions, he would often seek divine counsel and guidance by consulting the ephod, which was a resource God had provided for such use. Each time David consulted the ephod, the direction he received resulted in success and well-being.

Leaders are wise to seek God's guidance in important decisions. There are several divine resources available, including prayer, the Bible, the promptings of the Holy Spirit, and the counsel of godly women and men.

63. Not everyone who served your predecessor well will necessarily serve you well.

It is important to deal with "problem people" in ways that honor their past contributions, but in ways that also eliminate their potential for future damage.

Even though Solomon felt Abiathar deserved death, due to Abiathar's service to David he only removed Abiathar from the priesthood and eliminated his influence by sending him home to Anathoth (1 Kings 2:26). Solomon's action acknowledged the loyal service Abiathar had provided David and, at the same time, held him accountable for the disloyal service he had provided Solomon.

64. Leaders need to know the most appropriate ways to deal with individuals who would undermine their leadership.

While Abiathar's loyalty to David was evident, his lack of loyalty to Solomon was also evident. Abiathar had already made one decision designed to sabotage Solomon's kingship. He was not going to be given opportunity to make a second. Solomon could not afford to surround himself with people who would undermine his leadership.

Solomon did not put Abiathar to death, as he did Joab, Adonijah, and Shimei. While he had many options available to him, Solomon chose to exile Abiathar rather than to execute him. Thus, Solomon acknowledged the important contribution Abiathar had made during King David's reign, but also held him accountable for actions impacting Solomon's reign.

Those who would undermine your leadership will need to be dealt with wisely and fairly.

Questions for Leadership Development

1. How often, for what reasons, and in what ways do you seek divine guidance?

2. What are the influences that tend to undermine your leadership, and what are the best ways to deal with those influences?

3. What other leadership lessons can be derived from the story of Abiathar?

The Psalm

Psalm 24 is a processional psalm, commemorating when the ark was brought to Jerusalem.

Psalm 24

Of David. A psalm.

¹The earth is the Lord's, and everything in it,
 the world, and all who live in it;
²for he founded it on the seas
 and established it on the waters.
³Who may ascend the mountain of the Lord?
 Who may stand in his holy place?
⁴The one who has clean hands and a pure heart,
 who does not trust in an idol
 or swear by a false god.
⁵They will receive blessing from the Lord
 and vindication from God their Savior.
⁶Such is the generation of those who seek him,
 who seek your face, God of Jacob.
⁷Lift up your heads, you gates;
 be lifted up, you ancient doors,
 that the King of glory may come in.
⁸Who is this King of glory?
 The Lord strong and mighty,
 the Lord mighty in battle.
⁹Lift up your heads, you gates;
 lift them up, you ancient doors,
 that the King of glory may come in.
¹⁰Who is he, this King of glory?
 The Lord Almighty—
 he is the King of glory.

NINETEEN

MEPHIBOSHETH
THE ESSENCE OF GRACE: A PLACE AT THE TABLE

The Background

The story of Mephibosheth is told in 2 Samuel 9. He is also mentioned in 2 Samuel 4:4; 16:1-4; 19:24-30; 21:7-8.

The Story

Mephibosheth was the son of Jonathan, the only one the Bible tells us about. He was five years old when news of his family's death and defeat arrived at Jerusalem, causing such a panic that his nurse picked him up and began to flee. Unfortunately, she was so alarmed that she dropped the boy in her haste, breaking both of his legs and leaving him crippled for the rest of his life.

Now a young man, and knowing how most new kings dealt with potential rivals, Mephibosheth had decided to live in a remote area called Lo Debar, which literally means "no pastureland." He knew the history between David and Saul and wanted to stay as far away from David as possible.

Several years after Jonathan's death, however, David remembered the promise he had made to his friend Jonathan, to provide for his family in the case of his death. Ziba, who had been Saul's household servant, was summoned and asked if any of Jonathan's family members still existed. Even though David specified that his intention was to show kindness, Ziba may have assumed that David meant to do away with any of Saul's relatives who remained alive, which throughout history has often been a protocol of kingly succession. Ziba told David that one son of Jonathan was still alive—Mephibosheth—but stressed that he was "lame in both feet" and that he lived "at the house of Makir son of Ammiel in Lo Debar" (2 Sam. 9:3-4).

When Mephibosheth appeared before King David, he was probably afraid for his life. He limped into the palace figuring that he probably wouldn't live to limp out. As Mephibosheth bowed down in honor before the king, David said, "Don't be afraid, . . . for I will surely show you kindness for the sake of your father Jonathan" (2 Sam. 9:7). David then shared his intention to give Mephibosheth all the wealth and land that had belonged to his grandfather, Saul. Mephibosheth was also invited to eat at the king's table for the rest of his life.

Mephibosheth responded by observing his own unworthiness for such a magnanimous gesture. David blessed him even further by making Ziba the personal servant of Mephibosheth, assigning Ziba's household (Ziba had fifteen sons and twenty servants) to farm the land Mephibosheth had just received from David.

This part of the story ends with two statements made earlier being repeated—that Mephibosheth lived in Jerusalem (because he always ate at the king's table like one of the king's sons) and that he was lame in both feet. The statements paint a portrait of grace in action. Even though Mephibosheth had done and could do nothing to earn or deserve the goodness of the king, nonetheless he experienced the unmerited kindness of the king.

When David fled Jerusalem during Absalom's uprising, Ziba met him with transportation (donkeys) and provisions (bread, fruit, wine) for the journey. After Ziba told David that Mephibosheth was staying in Jerusalem in hopes that his grandfather's kingdom would be restored to him, David awarded Ziba all of Mephibosheth's inheritance.

As David returned to Jerusalem after Absalom's rebellion had been put down, he was surprised to be welcomed by none other than Mephibosheth, whose appearance (clothes unwashed, moustache untrimmed, feet unkempt) indicated that he had been observing a season of mourning for David. When asked why he had stayed in Jerusalem, Mephibosheth replied that he had been betrayed by Ziba, who had left him stranded in Jerusalem and who had slandered him by lying about his defection to Absalom.

Consistent with the magnanimous willingness to forgive wrongdoing that had marked David's journey back to Jerusalem, and perhaps exacerbated by a desire to avoid sullying his triumphant return by becoming mired in an investigation of exactly what happened between Mephibosheth and Ziba, David ordered that Saul's estate be divided between them. With a response that mirrored David's own generosity, Mephibosheth gushed that he was so glad David had survived the coup that he did not care if Ziba kept it all.[1]

Leadership Lessons

65. Each of us is in need of grace.

In many theological traditions, it is difficult to overemphasize the role of grace. In the captivating portrait of grace painted in the account of David and Mephibosheth, it is easy to see who we are in the story and who God is.

Like Mephibosheth, we have all been crippled by a fall and are unable to save ourselves, incapable of securing, earning, or even deserving our salvation. The fall that damaged us was the fall of Adam and Eve. As a result of that fall, each of us has been terribly disfigured by sin. We need a gracious King to save us and make us whole.

Like Mephibosheth, we have all found ourselves living in Lo Debar—a dry, arid wilderness far from the King. All of us have found ourselves in such a "far country." Unable to help ourselves, we have needed a gracious King who would seek us out and find us in our place of need.

When "success" has been achieved, and the rewards of such are being enjoyed, leaders would be wise to remember that the origin of every true blessing is grace, and grace alone. "Every good and perfect gift is from above" (James 1:17).

66. Each of us is offered grace.

When the King does find us in our lost estate, we know what we deserve, and it is not grace. But the King says, "Fear not. Don't be afraid." When those words appear in the Bible, they always introduce grace. "Fear not," says the King, "there is a place for you at my table."

David acted strictly out of loving-kindness. Mephibosheth had nothing to offer the king but gratitude. All Mephibosheth could do was gratefully receive the blessings and favor David presented him.

That's how it is with God. We bring so little—we are crippled in both feet—and he brings so much. And he invites us to the table. That's grace.

67. Each of us can extend grace.

What David did for Mephibosheth was a reflection of what God had done for David. God invites us not only to receive his grace but also to extend it to others. Each of us has the opportunity to extend to others the grace we have received ourselves. When we do, we become dispensers of that grace, channels of God's divine favor, lavishing on others the blessings overflowing from our lives. When we do, we discover that instead of the grace we have received being depleted, God's grace comes to us in even greater ways.

68. Leaders keep their promises and are careful what they promise.

Though David's covenant with Jonathan had been made years before and had not been witnessed, David still kept his promise. The fulfillment of his vow involved intentionality and sacrifice. David initiated the inquiry that led to the discovery of Mephibosheth and then presented Mephibosheth with property and goods that were David's own possessions.

Mellish notes that David:

reminds us of the importance of being people who keep our word. It is often easier for us to make promises to others than it is to keep them. Demonstrating the ability to fulfill our obligations and to keep our promises is a sign of maturity and character. We develop the reputation of being trustworthy and dependable when we remain steadfast in fulfilling our oaths. By remaining true to our word and fulfilling our commitments to others, we let people know that we value them and that they can rely on us.[2]

Questions for Leadership Development

1. How is the story of Mephibosheth similar to your story?

2. In what ways have you seen God's grace (God's favor that you could never earn or deserve) in your life?

3. Who are the people in your life to whom you can extend grace? What would that look like?

4. What other leadership lessons can be derived from the story of Mephibosheth?

The Psalm

In Psalm 103, David gives testimony to God's grace, praising him for his loving-kindness.

Psalm 103

Of David.
[1]Praise the LORD, my soul;
    all my inmost being, praise his holy name.
[2]Praise the LORD, my soul,
    and forget not all his benefits—
[3]who forgives all your sins
    and heals all your diseases,
[4]who redeems your life from the pit
    and crowns you with love and compassion,
[5]who satisfies your desires with good things
    so that your youth is renewed like the eagle's.
[6]The LORD works righteousness
    and justice for all the oppressed.
[7]He made known his ways to Moses,
    his deeds to the people of Israel:
[8]The LORD is compassionate and gracious,
    slow to anger, abounding in love.
[9]He will not always accuse,
    nor will he harbor his anger forever;
[10]he does not treat us as our sins deserve
    or repay us according to our iniquities.
[11]For as high as the heavens are above the earth,
    so great is his love for those who fear him;
[12]as far as the east is from the west,
    so far has he removed our transgressions from us.
[13]As a father has compassion on his children,
    so the LORD has compassion on those who fear him;
[14]for he knows how we are formed,
    he remembers that we are dust.

¹⁵The life of mortals is like grass,
>they flourish like a flower of the field;
¹⁶the wind blows over it and it is gone,
>and its place remembers it no more.
¹⁷But from everlasting to everlasting
>the LORD's love is with those who fear him,
>and his righteousness with their children's children—
¹⁸with those who keep his covenant
>and remember to obey his precepts.
¹⁹The LORD has established his throne in heaven,
>and his kingdom rules over all.
²⁰Praise the LORD, you his angels,
>you mighty ones who do his bidding,
>who obey his word.
²¹Praise the LORD, all his heavenly hosts,
>you his servants who do his will.
²²Praise the LORD, all his works
>everywhere in his dominion.
>Praise the LORD, my soul.

TWENTY

BATHSHEBA
FATAL ATTRACTION

The Background

The story of Bathsheba is told in 2 Samuel 11; 12:24; 1 Kings 1:11-31; 2:13-25; 1 Chronicles 3:5; Psalm 51.

The Story

One spring, David stayed in Jerusalem while Joab and the Israelite army went to war against the Ammonites. Though many would cite this as dereliction of duty or as complacency brought about by recent successes in battle, David's decision to become less of a field general and more of a commander-in-chief may not have been prudent, but it was not unusual. For centuries, armies have kept their top generals and leaders safe in the rear ranks or, where short distances were involved, even at home. The Ammonite capital of Rabbah was less than forty miles from Jerusalem, and David could monitor the battle through reports brought to him from his trusted general Joab. Messengers could be sent out from Jerusalem to alter strategy if necessary. Whatever his reasons, David found himself at home in his palace, with no active role to play in a campaign for the first time in a long time. For him, this would prove the wrong place at the wrong time. One night, David had difficulty going to sleep, so he got out of bed and took a warm, moonlit stroll on the terrace. From his rooftop vantage point he saw a beautiful woman bathing and sent someone to find out who she was. He was told she was "Bathsheba, the daughter of Eliam and the wife of Uriah the Hittite" (2 Sam. 11:3).

He shouldn't have had to ask who this woman was. He should have known the granddaughter of his chief adviser Ahithophel, especially when both her father Eliam[1] and her husband Uriah were part of the thirty elite warriors mentioned toward the end of 2 Samuel. None of this seems to have mattered to David though. He sent for her, and he slept with her (2 Sam. 11:4). The Bible doesn't record anything of Bathsheba's reaction to David's command, nor does it comment on her role in how events took place. She is not painted as a seductress, though she may have been a willing participant. She may have knowingly bathed in plain sight of the palace walls in order to tempt David; or she may not have realized that she could be seen at all and felt powerless against a king's decree. Whatever her inner thoughts, the Bible focuses solely on David's choices, clearly defining just whose decisions are being called to account.

Some time later, things went from bad to worse when David received word that Bathsheba was pregnant. In an effort to conceal his sin, David summoned Uriah from the battlefield in the hope that Uriah would re-consummate his marriage and believe the child was his own. David badly misjudged Uriah, who was unwilling to violate his personal code of warrior ethics. Rather than go home to his own bed, he slept at the entrance to the palace with the king's servants. Not even after David got him drunk would Uriah go home to his wife.

David then sent written orders to Joab (carried by Uriah) designed to result in Uriah's death. Uriah was to be placed in the front lines of the battle against Rabbah, where the fighting was the most dangerous, and then abandoned to the hands of the enemy. Joab carried out the orders and Uriah was killed.

After a respectable time of mourning had taken place, David made the newly widowed Bathsheba his wife, and she bore him a son. David's action displeased the Lord, who sent Nathan the prophet to confront the king with his sin. David at once confessed his sin and expressed sincere repentance. This first child of Bathsheba and David was struck with a severe illness and died a few days after birth. David accepted this outcome as his punishment. After the death of the child, David and Bathsheba had another child and named him Solomon.

Bathsheba is not mentioned again until the account of Solomon being crowned king. The prophet Nathan comes to tell her that Adonijah had set himself up to be king in the place of Solomon. As advised by Nathan, Bathsheba approached David with the news and asked him to crown Solomon king. After the news of Adonijah's activity was confirmed by Nathan, David announced that Solomon would indeed be king.

Later, Adonijah approached Bathsheba and asked if she would request of Solomon that Abishag be given to him in marriage. Solomon was incensed by the request and ordered the execution of Adonijah.

Bathsheba bore David four children: Shammua, Shobab, Nathan, and Solomon. All were born in Jerusalem.

Leadership Lessons

69. Leaders must, at all costs, avoid an entitlement mentality.[2]

David was a man after God's own heart.[3] Yet in one incident with Bathsheba he breaks over half of the Ten Commandments. This incident becomes, at his death, the only liability charged against him.[4]

Throughout his rise to the throne of Israel and during his reign, a hallmark of David's kingship is that he never felt entitled to the throne. We see this most clearly in his dealings with Saul and with Absalom. However, in this incident, David apparently felt entitled to something that should have been considered off-limits to him.

Feelings of entitlement are particularly troubling temptations for leaders because these feelings can lead them to abuse the positions and power with which they have been entrusted. When leaders begin to say, or to think, "I deserve this" or "I've earned this" or "Others with my responsibilities enjoy this," they are positioned for a dangerous fall.

No matter what position of leadership you have, privilege will likely become a temptation. No one is immune from the temptation to acquire inappropriate perks. David's fall followed years of success, which likely lessened his dependence on God and increased his enjoyment of the growing benefits associated with his office.

Beware of the entitlement mentality and the tendency toward moral laxity that often accompanies prosperity and success.

70. Vision can be both a blessing and a curse.

David's downfall began with a look—a lingering look that grew into lust.

Much has been written about vision—the desired future that a leader needs to see. Much more needs to be written about what a leader needs to guard against seeing. Job recognized when he wrote, "I made a covenant with my eyes not to look lustfully at a young woman" (Job 31:1).

Vision is one of the primary characteristics of a good leader. "Be careful little eyes what you see" is valuable advice, lest an asset become a liability.

71. Leaders must avoid viewing individuals as objects to be used for their own benefits.

David was attracted to Bathsheba. He was interested in her as an object of physical beauty rather than as a person of worth. When David inquires as to her identity, the description of Bathsheba becomes significant. She is identified in terms of her relationship to her father and her husband. Mellish observes, "In essence, Bathsheba was not just an object to be conquered or manipulated; she was a valuable human being as both a daughter and a wife."[5]

When leaders treat people as objects to be used for a desired end, they disregard and disrespect the worth of an individual. Such leaders abuse people by treating them as a means to an end or as objects to fulfill desire, rather than as people to be valued and loved.

Good leaders protect the rights of others, rather than ignoring them. They recognize the feelings of others, rather than dismissing them.

72. Isolation is the breeding ground for temptation.

David was in a season of isolation when he experienced the temptation that would lead to his moral failure. He had separated himself from those he was typically around and had allowed his mind and attention to disengage from his duty and his responsibilities.

David's isolation was the birthing ground for temptation. We were created for community. Leaders who exist in community are less prone to moral failure. Healthy connections are important to our well-being. When you are accountable to someone—a spouse, a friend, a Christian counselor—such accountability can provide an antidote to temptation. Simply admitting the temptation to an accountability partner can rob temptation of its power.[6] Be accountable to someone. Heed the promptings of the Holy Spirit. Pray for strength to overcome temptation. Avoid isolation.

73. There is a fatal progression with sin.

The story of David and Bathsheba paints a telling picture of the downward spiral of sin. The steps are clearly evident, beginning with *imagination*. David saw Bathsheba, and then he stared at Bathsheba. Sin always begins in the mind. First, Satan gets our attention. The next step is *investigation*. David found out about Bathsheba. What he learned should have put an end to his imagination. It did not. Imagination and investigation have given birth to *temptation*. The next step is *gratification*. David willfully commits adultery. The next step is *trepidation*. Bathsheba comes to David and says, "I am pregnant," which leads to trepidation— the anxious fear that what was done in secret is coming to light. The last step is *separation* and death. Sin always has consequences. Something dies. A lot of things die in the story between David and Bathsheba. Faithfulness dies. A marriage dies. A man dies. A baby dies.

74. Reality cannot be ignored.

It is hard to believe that God would want this story in his Book. It is embarrassing. But the Bible is honest about who we are and what we have done and who God is and what he has done. David was a mighty warrior, but the greatest battles are fought on the inside; this was a battle David lost. Jonathan Kirsch observes, "King David chooses pleasure over piety, and both king and country will pay a terrible price."[7]

75. God's grace is greater than a leader's sin.

David's sin was great, but God's mercy is greater. God did not simply ignore David's sin. Rather, when David repented and turned away from his evil behavior, God responded to such repentance with forgiveness and mercy. He sends Nathan to David a second time with a word, not of accusation, but of encouragement. The second child born to David and Bathsheba is to be called Jedidiah, which means "loved of the Lord."[8] God has not abandoned David because of his gross sinfulness. Rather, God continues to love him.

The only appropriate response of a leader to personal sin is confession and repentance, and the sooner the better.

Questions for Leadership Development

1. On what occasions have you become aware of your own entitlement mentality?

2. What other temptation(s) are you presently battling?

3. How are you guarding your heart?

4. What other leadership lessons can be derived from the story of Bathsheba?

The Psalm

The story of David's adultery sets up the context for the penitential Psalm 51, also known as "Miserere" ("Have mercy on me, O God"). Confession is the first step of repentance and the first step toward restoration. David was an adulterer and a murderer. He finally got what was coming to him: forgiveness.

Psalm 51

For the director of music. A psalm of David. When the prophet Nathan came to him after David had committed adultery with Bathsheba.
¹Have mercy on me, O God,
according to your unfailing love;
according to your great compassion
blot out my transgressions.
²Wash away all my iniquity
and cleanse me from my sin.
³For I know my transgressions,
and my sin is always before me.
⁴Against you, you only, have I sinned
and done what is evil in your sight;
so you are right in your verdict
and justified when you judge.
⁵Surely I was sinful at birth,
sinful from the time my mother conceived me.
⁶Yet you desired faithfulness even in the womb;
you taught me wisdom in that secret place.
⁷Cleanse me with hyssop, and I will be clean;
wash me, and I will be whiter than snow.
⁸Let me hear joy and gladness;
let the bones you have crushed rejoice.
⁹Hide your face from my sins
and blot out all my iniquity.
¹⁰Create in me a pure heart, O God,
and renew a steadfast spirit within me.

[11]Do not cast me from your presence
    or take your Holy Spirit from me.
[12]Restore to me the joy of your salvation
    and grant me a willing spirit, to sustain me.
[13]Then I will teach transgressors your ways,
    so that sinners will turn back to you.
[14]Deliver me from the guilt of bloodshed, O God,
    you who are God my Savior,
    and my tongue will sing of your righteousness.
[15]Open my lips, Lord,
    and my mouth will declare your praise.
[16]You do not delight in sacrifice, or I would bring it;
    you do not take pleasure in burnt offerings.
[17]My sacrifice, O God, is a broken spirit;
    a broken and contrite heart
    you, God, will not despise.
[18]May it please you to prosper Zion,
    to build up the walls of Jerusalem.
[19]Then you will delight in the sacrifices of the righteous,
    in burnt offerings offered whole;
    then bulls will be offered on your altar.

TWENTY-ONE

URIAH
SEMPER FIDELIS

The Background

The story of Uriah is told in 2 Samuel 11 and 12. He is also mentioned in 2 Samuel 23:39; 1 Kings 15:5; 1 Chronicles 11:41; Matthew 1:6.

The Story

It is hard to imagine a more noble and loyal individual than Uriah. Although a Hittite by birth, he was apparently at least a second generation Jew by religion, for his name contains the "iah" suffix for Jehovah and means the flame (or light) of Jehovah. Five other Israelites in the Bible bear the same name. Like his father-in-law, Eliam, he was one of David's "mighty men," an exclusive, elite group of warriors that made up David's bodyguard. Uriah was among "the best of the best"—faithful, loyal, duty-bound—the kind of man you want on your side.

Uriah was married to a beautiful woman named Bathsheba, from a well-known family, and when Uriah went off to fight battles, Bathsheba stayed home in Jerusalem. One spring, Uriah went off with Joab and the rest of the army to fight the Ammonites. It was a successful campaign, culminating with the siege of Rabbah. It would only be a matter of time before the city fell and the army was back home.

During the siege, Uriah was summoned to Jerusalem to report to King David, who had recently learned that his tryst with Bathsheba had resulted in her pregnancy. When Uriah arrived, David inquired about the status of Joab, the status of the troops, and the status of the siege. Then David sent Uriah home—along with a gift—in hopes that Uriah would sleep with Bathsheba, which would provide a convenient explanation for her pregnancy. But Uriah stayed at the palace gates with David's servants that night. Upon learning that he did not go home, David asked Uriah why he had not gone to see Bathsheba. Uriah responded that he could not in good conscience enjoy the pleasures of home while Joab and the troops slept in the open country.

David had him stay one more day. That evening David got Uriah drunk, thinking Uriah's resolve would be weakened and that he would go home to Bathsheba. But Uriah slept a second night at the palace gate. David's plan to see Bathsheba's pregnancy attributed to Uriah's visit having failed, he now resorted to a plan to eliminate Uriah.

The next morning, David sent Uriah back to the battle with a confidential message for Joab. The message—Uriah's death sentence—ordered Joab to put Uriah in the front lines, where the fighting was the fiercest, and then to withdraw, leaving Uriah isolated. The enemy made quick work of him.

The next battle report that David received from Joab contained news of victory at Rabbah. However, the message contained this line: "Moreover, your servant Uriah the Hittite is dead" (2 Sam. 11:24).

Uriah's passing was mourned by Bathsheba, and after an acceptable time David took her as his wife.

Soon, the prophet Nathan made David's sins very plain to him, accusing him of using the sword of the Ammonites to strike down Uriah and take his wife.

Uriah is not forgotten. Often, the Bible refers to Bathsheba as "Uriah's wife" rather than mentioning her by name. It is the name of Uriah, not Bathsheba, that is mentioned in Matthew's genealogy of Jesus.

Leadership Lessons

76. The contrast between loyalty and disloyalty—between faithfulness and unfaithfulness—is stark.

Uriah provides a great example of loyalty and faithfulness. His singleness of purpose and zeal for the Lord's cause was exemplary, as was his strong sense of duty and identification with his fellow soldiers.

Uriah shows himself to be a loyal, decent, and courageous man—a man who knows about duty. Pinsky notes, "Uriah, though drunk and possibly overwhelmed by David's company, declines to betray his vow. (Nor does he betray loyal solidarity with his celibate comrades, still at the battlefront.) He does not sleep with Bathsheba."[1] When Uriah couldn't bring himself to enjoy a night with his wife while his buddies were off at war, David knew he was in even more trouble. This sin was not going to be easy to hide.

The Thirty mighty men—the fiercest and most elite fighting men in David's army—would have done anything for him. But David repays that loyalty and faithfulness with disloyalty and un-faithfulness.

The differences are stark. The situation of David's soldiers—sleeping in the open fields—is in stark contrast with the situation of David, who was enjoying the pleasures of the palace. Uriah refused to enjoy pleasures not available to his brothers-in-arms. David was willing to take in his arms pleasures not meant for him. Uriah, the drunken soldier, is more noble than David, the sober king. The man David fought alongside on the battlefront became a victim of David's lust on the home front. There is also a stark difference between Joab and Uriah. Not only did Uriah display loyalty to his king and the nation, but he also showed a fierce personal loyalty to Joab. How ironic it is that Joab is the one who is commissioned to arrange for the death of Uriah.

Loyalty and faithfulness are key to spiritual, familial, and organizational health. When they are replaced by disloyalty and unfaithfulness, the health of the organization, the family, and the soul of a person are placed at risk.

77. Bad decisions breed bad decisions.[2]

The bad decisions began to pile up for David. They have a tendency to do that. Bad decisions breed more bad decisions, especially when we try to cover things up. David knew who Bathsheba was—that she was the wife of someone else. His decision to sleep with her was not only bad but sinful. David knew Bathsheba's husband, Uriah, would not be happy about his wife carrying someone else's baby. So David sent orders for her husband to come back for a little rest and relaxation. He thought for sure Uriah would want to be with his wife, but the faithful husband proved to be more noble than the unfaithful king. David's next decision to have Uriah killed was also not only bad but sinful. Pinsky suggests that the killing of Uriah was "apparently motivated less by desire to have Bathsheba for a wife than by something like the avoidance of an ugly paternity suit."[3] The bad decisions were piling up.

Up to this point David had won all kinds of battles. He was a warrior. But in this case it is not Philistines or Amalekites, political rebels or rebellious sons he has to defeat. His biggest enemy is himself.

David could have immediately admitted what he had done with Bathsheba. He could have begged Uriah's forgiveness and come clean with the whole thing. Instead, he chose to get rid of Uriah. David abused his authority and disgraced his position.

Too often, leaders attempt to cover up initial transgressions by committing more transgressions, lies upon lies, sins upon sins. The end result is much more damaging and harmful than would have been the case if the leader had recognized the failure, admit-

SEMPER FIDELIS

ted the transgression, sought forgiveness, and made restitution in the beginning.

78. Sooner or later, a leader's sin is always found out.

David, like many others, thought he could cover up his sin. Sin functions at its highest efficiency when it operates in isolation or secrecy. But the day came when David's sin was brought to light and seen in all its ugliness. Cover-ups do not remain covered up indefinitely.

Sin never stays permanently hidden. It is easy to name leaders who have learned this lesson the hard way. Every generation has seen the careers of political, military, ministry, and corporate leaders ruined, families irreparably damaged, and reputations tarnished when sins thought hidden come to light.

"You may be sure that your sin will find you out" (Num. 32:23).

79. When sin is found out, there will be complications and consequences.

David's sin created unwanted complications and far-reaching consequences. The longer sin goes, the messier it gets. Mellish notes, "After David's tryst with Bathsheba and the murder of Uriah, his life was never the same. David was plagued with both internal family matters and political upheaval."[4] Though God gives grace to live with the consequences, there are still consequences. Some of the consequences were immediate—guilt, regret, innocent people getting hurt, trust being violated, and other individuals being corrupted. Some consequences were far-reaching—the loss of respect in his kingdom that led to future leadership problems, the loss of fighting men and morale among his troops, to name a few. Still another consequence in response to David's conduct toward Bathsheba may have been Ahithophel's desertion of David at the time of Absalom's rebellion.

Have you ever known a leader who has fallen? All those stories are tragic, but some become stories of grace. All are stories of character and integrity rejected; some become stories of character and integrity restored.

Leaders are wise to minimize the opportunity for temptation. The best way to survive an ambush is to avoid an ambush.[5] When it comes to temptation, the Bible is quite clear on the appropriate strategy, and that strategy is to run away, to flee temptation. Another strategy is to consider the consequences. For every sinful thought, ask yourself, "Is this worth it? Will this be worth it to me, to my family, and to my future?"

80. The sin of one leader can result in the suffering of many other people.

Sinful action always results in "collateral damage," which is plainly seen in David's sins against Bathsheba and Uriah. Uriah was not the only casualty in David's home-front failures.

In the same way that the wake of a large ship can create turmoil for and even capsize smaller vessels, so the sins of a leader have a ripple effect that negatively impact other people, even in succeeding generations. David's sin impacted Bathsheba, who suffered the loss of a husband and a child, and one cannot but wonder what emotional price she paid. David's sin impacted Uriah's family, who not only lost a son, brother, and husband, but who must have also lost a great deal of respect for the kingship. David's sin impacted his army, who suffered loss of both men and morale in the battle in which Uriah was killed. In addition to the mourning of Bathsheba for her son, the family members of those other soldiers killed in action also mourned their loss.

David's sin impacted his own family. Absalom and Adonijah—who both would later also attempt to take what was not theirs—were impacted if not influenced by their father's sin.

Leaders should never think that their sin will not matter, or that they will be the only ones affected. Our sinful actions can have a negative impact not only on those around us but also on generations that follow us.

Questions for Leadership Development

1. What evidences of loyalty and faithfulness are there in your organization?

2. How can leaders guard against their own abuse of power?

3. To whom do you need to remain loyal?

4. What other leadership lessons can be derived from the story of Uriah?

The Psalm

One of the penitential psalms, Psalm 38 is a psalm that David wrote after the murder of Uriah, in which he repents of his sins with Bathsheba and Uriah.

Psalm 38

A psalm of David. A petition.

¹LORD, do not rebuke me in your anger
   or discipline me in your wrath.
²Your arrows have pierced me,
   and your hand has come down on me.
³Because of your wrath there is no health in my body;
   there is no soundness in my bones because of my sin.
⁴My guilt has overwhelmed me
   like a burden too heavy to bear.
⁵My wounds fester and are loathsome
   because of my sinful folly.
⁶I am bowed down and brought very low;
   all day long I go about mourning.
⁷My back is filled with searing pain;
   there is no health in my body.
⁸I am feeble and utterly crushed;
   I groan in anguish of heart.
⁹All my longings lie open before you, Lord;
   my sighing is not hidden from you.
¹⁰My heart pounds, my strength fails me;
   even the light has gone from my eyes.
¹¹My friends and companions avoid me because of my wounds;
   my neighbors stay far away.
¹²Those who want to kill me set their traps,
   those who would harm me talk of my ruin;
   all day long they scheme and lie.
¹³I am like the deaf, who cannot hear,
   like the mute, who cannot speak;

[14]I have become like one who does not hear,
  whose mouth can offer no reply.
[15]Lord, I wait for you;
  you will answer, Lord my God.
[16]For I said, "Do not let them gloat
  or exalt themselves over me when my feet slip."
[17]For I am about to fall,
  and my pain is ever with me.
[18]I confess my iniquity;
  I am troubled by my sin.
[19]Many have become my enemies without cause;
  those who hate me without reason are numerous.
[20]Those who repay my good with evil
  lodge accusations against me,
  though I seek only to do what is good.
[21]Lord, do not forsake me;
  do not be far from me, my God.
[22]Come quickly to help me,
  my Lord and my Savior.

— TWENTY-TWO —

NATHAN
WHO SPEAKS TRUTH INTO YOUR LIFE?

The Background

The story of Nathan is told in 2 Samuel 7; 12; 1 Kings 1; 1 Chronicles 17; Psalm 51:1. He is also mentioned in 2 Samuel 23:36; 1 Kings 4:5; 1 Chronicles 11:38; 29:29; 2 Chronicles 9:29; 29:25; Zechariah 12:12.

The Story

Nathan[1] was one of three prophets who speaks into David's life (the others being Samuel and Gad). We first hear of Nathan when David shared with the prophet his dream of building the temple. David had brought the ark of God to Jerusalem, but it bothered him that the ark was housed in a tent while he lived in a beautiful palace. Initially, Nathan encouraged David to proceed with his plans, but that night Nathan had a dream in which God told him that David was not the one to construct the temple, because his hands were so bloodstained. Nathan was instructed to reassure David of the special favor he enjoyed and that the line of kingly succession would not depart from his family. But David's successor would be the one to build the temple. Nathan reported this to David, and David responded by praising the Lord for his goodness.

Nathan's next appearance is abrupt, having been sent by the Lord to confront David with his sin in the matter of Uriah and Bathsheba. Nathan told David the story of two men, one rich and one poor. When a guest stopped by for hospitality at the home of the rich man (who had plenty of cattle and sheep) the rich man took the poor man's only lamb (the family pet) and butchered it for their dinner. David became livid, insisting the rich man was worthy of death and demanding he pay restitution as well as a steep penalty. David's sin became very clear when Nathan confronted him with the words, "You are the man!" (2 Sam. 12:7).

To David's credit he immediately acknowledges his guilt. No excuses. No alibis. No rationalization. Simply and genuinely David confesses, "I have sinned against the LORD" (v. 13). He repents to God and is so aware of his guilt that he willingly accepts his punishment in advance of knowing it.

Nathan's response was full of grace as well as consequence. His words of forgiveness contain a prophecy of catastrophe and family tragedy that await David. There is also a hint of Absalom's future action.

After Nathan returned to his home, the son born to David and Bathsheba took ill as Nathan had foretold and died seven days later. David comforted Bathsheba in her grief and another child was born to them. This son was named Solomon, but God sent word through Nathan that the boy was to be named Jedidiah, which means "loved by the Lord."

Nathan appears on the scene once again when Adonijah sets himself up as successor to David's throne. It is by Nathan's intervention that Solomon rises to the kingship instead of Adonijah. Nathan, along with Zadok and Benaiah, were the members of David's cabinet who did not support Adonijah in his bid for the kingship. While Adonijah's coronation party was in full swing, Nathan and Bathsheba tactfully approached David with the news of Adonijah's coup. David then sent Zadok, Nathan, and Benaiah to Gihon to anoint Solomon king over Israel.

Leadership Lessons

81. It may be that your vision will be accomplished by your successor, not you.

Building the temple was David's idea. The dream was David's dream. The plan was David's plan. The blueprints were David's blueprints. The resources were accumulated by David. Yet, it was Solomon who built the temple. What David did not have was God's blessing upon the undertaking. It must have been difficult for Nathan to go back to King David and reverse his course. Building the temple was a great idea, but it wasn't God's plan. Swindoll writes, "One of the hardest things to hear is that God is going to use someone else to accomplish something you thought was your objective."[2]

David's response was exemplary. He praised God for the promise that his kingly line would never end and began to make preparations that would make it easier for Solomon to bring the vision to reality. His response was unselfish, glorified God, and benefitted the kingdom.

God did not allow David to build the temple, but he did allow David to make preparations for Solomon's building of the temple. What seems to have been most important to David was not that he be the one to build the temple but that the temple be built. David positioned Solomon for success by giving him his blessing and ensured the needed resources were available.

Your dream may only become reality under the leadership of your successor. If the good of the organization or ministry one is leading is more important than one's ego, a response like David's will be possible. Making preparations that will help ensure the success of your successor is the sign of a mature and responsible leader.

Your dream may become your successor's greatest achievement.

82. Every leader needs someone to speak truth into his or her life.

When one gains a position of influence and authority, it almost always means that fewer people are willing to tell you the truth. This happens for several reasons, including a desire to impress the leader, to gain the favor of the leader, to avoid the leader's negative response to the truth, or because people genuinely hold the leader in such high esteem that they think the leader's actions must be right.

God provided just about every king with a prophet to keep him honest, or at least so he would be without excuse. Saul had Samuel, Ahab had Elijah, Hezekiah had Isaiah, Herod had John the Baptist, and David had Nathan. Nathan told David the truth tactfully, privately, and effectively. He drew David in with a story. Disarmed, David walked right into the truth.

While many leaders are prone to avoid conflict, one cannot diminish the importance of confrontation. We all need people in our lives who will tell us the truth. Kings need prophets to keep them honest, just as leaders need truth-tellers to keep them honest.

Kirsch eloquently describes this dynamic. "Just as Saul deferred to Samuel, and David deferred to Nathan, the kings of Judah and Israel always found themselves confronted and condemned by fearless truth-tellers who cared not at all for the trappings of royal authority, or, for that matter, the equally ornate trappings of the priesthood that presided over the Temple."[3]

If God has called you to confront sin, do so humbly, courageously, and artfully. Do so at the right time (diplomatically), in the right way (tactfully), with the right words (truthfully), and with the right attitude (humbly).

Unfortunately, it is possible to build an organizational structure, or to create an organizational culture, in which it is all but impossible for a prophet to be heard, or to survive. There may be times when you need to confront others with their sin. Or, there may be times when others need to confront you with your sin. If so, may you have the courage of Nathan in the one case and the honesty of David in the other.

It is noteworthy that the third child born to David and Bathsheba was given the name Nathan. The first child died before a name was given, the second was named Solomon, and the third child was named Nathan. Very likely the name was chosen in honor of Nathan the prophet, who remained a trusted adviser to both David and Bathsheba.

83. While forgiveness will remove the guilt of sin, the consequences of sin almost always remain.

Leaders reap what they sow. If they sow righteousness, they harvest the benefits of righteousness; if they sow sin, they reap the consequences of their transgression.

Hidden sin does not stay secret forever. When confronted by Nathan, to David's credit he immediately made an open admission and acknowledged his guilt in confession. Repentance is the beginning of spiritual healing and restoration. While the guilt of his sin was removed, David would have to live with the bitter result of his transgression. God forgave him, but Uriah was still dead. Bathsheba was still pregnant. The child she was carrying would still die a week after its birth. The consequences of David's sin also included the negative example he provided to his children.

Sin has consequences. Whether you are king or pauper, sin carries ramifications. Unfortunately, the sins of a leader almost always affect a lot more people than the leader alone. Sins can be forgiven, but the consequence of those sins is bitter fruit that is often harvested over many seasons.

Questions for Leadership Development

1. Who speaks truth into your life?

2. What is your typical response when "the truth" is bad news?

3. How would you react to the news that your great plan will be accomplished by another?

4. What other leadership lessons can be derived from the story of Nathan?

WHO SPEAKS TRUTH INTO YOUR LIFE?

The Psalm

One of the penitential psalms, Psalm 32 is a psalm that David wrote after the murder of Uriah, in which he repents of his sins with Bathsheba and Uriah. God used Nathan to convict David of his sin.

Psalm 32

Of David. A maskil.
¹Blessed is the one
    whose transgressions are forgiven,
    whose sins are covered.
²Blessed is the one
    whose sin the LORD does not count against them
    and in whose spirit is no deceit.
³When I kept silent,
    my bones wasted away
    through my groaning all day long.
⁴For day and night
    your hand was heavy on me;
 my strength was sapped
    as in the heat of summer.
⁵Then I acknowledged my sin to you
    and did not cover up my iniquity.
 I said, "I will confess
    my transgressions to the LORD."
 And you forgave
    the guilt of my sin.
⁶Therefore let all the faithful pray to you
    while you may be found;
 surely the rising of the mighty waters
    will not reach them.
⁷You are my hiding place;
    you will protect me from trouble
    and surround me with songs of deliverance.

⁸I will instruct you and teach you in the way you should go;
    I will counsel you with my loving eye on you.
⁹Do not be like the horse or the mule,
    which have no understanding
 but must be controlled by bit and bridle
    or they will not come to you.
¹⁰Many are the woes of the wicked,
    but the Lord's unfailing love
    surrounds the one who trusts in him.
¹¹Rejoice in the Lord and be glad, you righteous;
    sing, all you who are upright in heart!

TWENTY-THREE

ABSALOM
BETRAYAL OF THE WORST KIND

The Background

The story of Absalom is told in 2 Samuel 13—19. He is also mentioned in 2 Samuel 3:3; 20:6; 1 Kings 1:6; 2:7, 28; 1 Chronicles 3:2; 2 Chronicles 11:20, 21; Psalm 3:1.

The Story

Absalom was born in Hebron, the third son of David. His mother was Maakah, daughter of Talmai, king of Geshur. Absalom was handsome, personable, privileged, and excessively ambitious. Heir apparent to the throne, he could not wait to become king and attempted to hasten the occasion by seizing rule from his father, David.

Absalom's story begins with the assault of his sister, Tamar, by their lecherous half-brother, Amnon. Amnon pretended to be ill and requested to be cared for by Tamar, who was striking in her beauty. David granted the request, and when Amnon found himself alone with his sister, he raped her, and then threw her out of the house. When Absalom learned of the assault, he took his sister Tamar, now "a desolate woman," into his own home to provide for her.

David's lack of action in response to this offense may have been the beginning of Absalom's rebellion. Though David was "furious" (2 Sam. 13:21) when he heard of the rape of his daughter, he did nothing to bring about justice. No doubt, Absalom took note of this and in time reached the conclusion that if his father would not bring a son guilty of rape to justice, he might not bring a son guilty of murder to justice.

For two years Absalom nursed his hatred for Amnon and plotted his treachery. Then Absalom set in motion his plan to avenge the rape of his sister. David granted Absalom's request to have Amnon and the rest of the king's sons join Absalom for a celebration at sheep-shearing time. At the high point of the party Absalom gave the word to his men, and Amnon was murdered. The rest of the king's sons fled in fear. The first report David received—that all his sons had been murdered—was erroneous. The second report, this one brought by Jonadab—that only Amnon was dead—was factual. Not only had Absalom avenged the rape of his sister, but he had eliminated the first in line for the throne as well.

Absalom fled, seeking safe haven with his maternal grandfather, Talmai, the king of Geshur, where he stayed for three years. Just as David had done nothing about the rape of Tamar, he did nothing about the murder of Amnon. Rather, he "longed to go to Absalom, for he was consoled concerning Amnon's death" (v. 39).

After three years had passed, Joab devised a ruse by which David was persuaded to recall Absalom. It was another two years before Absalom was restored to favor, and that only after Absalom, by a trick of his own, moved Joab to intercede with the king.

Meanwhile, Absalom's skillful manipulation and aspirations for the throne began to surface. He paraded about with a great entourage, rallied followers, and subtly suggested to those seeking justice how he would govern in the best interests of the people. While David found it difficult to discipline Absalom, others found it difficult to resist him. "In all Israel there was not a man so highly praised for his handsome appearance as Absalom. From the top of his head to the sole of his foot there was no blemish in him. Whenever he cut the hair of his head . . . its weight was two hundred shekels by the royal standard" (2 Sam. 14:25-26). Because all three of his sons had died, Absalom constructed a monument to himself, ironically, in the "King's Dale," to ensure his legacy.

In the fortieth year[1] of David's reign, Absalom's conspiracy was launched. Under the guise of visiting Hebron to worship, Absalom proclaimed himself king and began to build his coalition. Hebron had been the capital of Judah when David began his reign and was Absalom's birthplace.

The gravity of the situation was immediately apparent to David, and the king hastily fled Jerusalem. David's poignant flight from the capital was accompanied by the intense loyalty of true friends and the disappointing betrayal of false ones. David's valued adviser Ahithophel joined the conspiracy. The priests Zadok and Abiathar proved true and were sent back to Jerusalem as spies along with Hushai the Arkite, whose job was to feign loyalty to Absalom, that he might help David "by frustrating Ahithophel's advice" (2 Sam. 15:34).

Upon entering Jerusalem, Ahithophel suggested that conducting a public orgy with David's concubines on the roof of the palace would leave no doubt as to Absalom's resolve to take the throne. Ahithophel then advised Absalom to attack David immediately, before he could gather a large following. Hushai advised delay, so that all the military strength of the kingdom could be gathered under command of Absalom himself, to make certain of having a large enough force to defeat the experienced David and his devoted soldiers.

Absalom rejected Ahithophel's advice, which was exactly what David had prayed would happen. The delay gave David time to escape and muster his forces. When the armies did meet in the forest of Ephraim, Absalom's men were soundly defeated.

During the battle, Absalom, riding on a mule, was caught by his hair in the branches of an oak. The mule kept going and left Absalom dangling. He was soon found and killed by Joab and his men, even though David had forbidden anyone to harm Absalom.

Absalom was disgracefully buried in a pit and covered with a heap of stones in the woods where he fell.

David was shattered by the news. Had it not been for Joab's warning, David's excessive grief over Absalom's death may have cost him the kingdom. The wailing of David—"O my son Absalom! My son, my son Absalom! If only I had died instead of you" (2 Sam. 18:33)—over the loss of his son had stolen away the congratulations the army deserved for their victory. As Buechner notes, "The boy was the thorn in his flesh, but he was also the apple of his eye."[2]

Leadership Lessons

84. Leadership begins at home.

Parenting requires involvement. David was an important, powerful, and busy man. He was a successful king. But he failed at fatherhood because of his lack of attention to his parenting responsibilities. He literally let his son "get away with murder."

Success in other arenas of life (business, politics, sports, entertainment, church) does not automatically mean success at home. The pressure and demands of success in the other arenas of life can make success at home even more difficult, making it all the more important that leaders remember the primacy of responsibility at home.

David was not the first leader in Israel who failed to discipline his own children. One of the reasons Israel had a king to begin with was because of Samuel's failure to discipline his own children, a shortcoming also evidenced in Eli's relationship with his own sons.

While leaders may not be able to determine the actions of their own children, they do have opportunity to provide a positive influence on their children's behavior. Parents are also responsible for holding their children accountable for their actions, especially while those children are under their supervision. It may be difficult to be objective where family is concerned, but for a parent to overlook the immoral behavior of a child is to ignore a most important responsibility of parenting. One can only surmise how the trajectory of Absalom's life would have differed if David had responded appropriately to the rape of Tamar and to the murder of Amnon.

Many of the responsibilities of leadership can be accomplished by others—by those who have similar training, giftedness, or experience. However, no one but you can fulfill the responsibility you have as a spouse or a parent.

85. Unbridled ambition is disaster in the making.

That Absalom was popular with the populace is beyond question. His charm was magnetic; his attractiveness was alluring. But alas, "to be popular is not to be chosen."[3]

Absalom's lack of discipline, coupled with his excessive ambition, led to tragedy. This is inevitably the case. Absalom's gifts were significant; his potential was unlimited. What he lacked was someone to help shape him by modeling personal responsibility and integrity and holding him accountable for the same.

It is critical that leaders realize the important role accountability plays in the development of healthy ambition. This is a valuable lesson for leaders to learn, both for their personal benefit, and for the benefit of those they serve.

86. Nothing reveals a leader's heart like the response to betrayal.

Your reaction to threats, be they real or perceived, will reveal your heart. As we have seen in earlier chapters, there is a marked difference between the way Saul responded to the perceived but illusory threat that David posed to the throne and the way David responded to the very real threat to the throne that Absalom posed.[4] In his responses to both Saul and Absalom, David did not grasp the throne. Rather, he trusted God to ensure the throne was ruled by the right man.

Godly leaders respond to betrayal, not with a note of vindictiveness, but with a certain trust in God. David's response to

Absalom's betrayal revealed that he was "a man after God's own heart."[5]

87. Decisiveness and the ability to appropriately allocate available resources can be key to survival.

It has been said that the number one responsibility of a leader is to define reality. At the onset of Absalom's revolt, David very quickly grasped reality and took decisive action. He accurately assessed the threat, took steps to protect both himself and others from the threat, and deployed the available human resources in ways that provided the greatest benefit.

Organizations thrive when leaders make good decisions in a timely manner. Organizations suffer not only when leaders make poor decisions but also when leaders fail to make any decision at all. Mohler observes, "Indecisiveness is one of history's greatest leadership killers."[6]

88. Assets can become liabilities.

Absalom's thick, luxuriant hair was an asset. It was a source of admiration of others, but it was also a source of pride for Absalom. Ultimately, Absalom's hair became his downfall. One of his defining attributes became a deadly snare.

A leader's pride can result in strengths becoming weaknesses and assets becoming liabilities.

89. Leaders who erect monuments in honor of themselves seldom have monuments in their honor erected by others.

Absalom, wanting to ensure his legacy, erected a monument to himself in the King's Dale. No other monument was ever constructed to honor him, and he was ignobly buried in the woods in a pit covered with rocks. His self-built monument does not survive. What does survive is his legacy of betrayal.

Shameless self-promotion is all too common—and usually has tragic consequences.

Questions for Leadership Development

1. How does a leader recognize the difference between unbridled ambition and healthy ambition, and is it possible for a leader to help someone transition from unbridled ambition to healthy ambition?

2. How does a leader best deal with treachery and betrayal?

3. What are the ways leaders can develop the ability to define reality and grasp the significance and potential consequences of current events on the organization they lead?

4. How can a leader ensure that God-given, personal assets do not become liabilities?

5. When threatened, is your first inclination to eliminate the threat (problem) or to remove the threat-maker (person)?

6. What other leadership lessons can be derived from the story of Absalom?

The Psalm

Psalm 3 is a psalm of David, written when he fled from his son Absalom.

Psalm 3

[1]LORD, how many are my foes!
  How many rise up against me!
[2]Many are saying of me,
  "God will not deliver him."
[3]But you, LORD, are a shield around me,
  my glory, the One who lifts my head high.
[4]I call out to the LORD,
  and he answers me from his holy mountain.
[5]I lie down and sleep;
  I wake again, because the LORD sustains me.
[6]I will not fear though tens of thousands
  assail me on every side.
[7]Arise, LORD!
  Deliver me, my God!
Strike all my enemies on the jaw;
  break the teeth of the wicked.
[8]From the LORD comes deliverance.
  May your blessing be on your people.

TWENTY-FOUR

ABISHAG
GROWING OLD, GROWING COLD

The Background

The story of Abishag is told in 1 Kings 1—2.

The Story

As people grow old, their ability to stay warm often wanes. The elderly frequently seek increased warmth—warmer homes, warmer hearts, warmer memories. The same was true of David. When he became old, he became cold. Not even a pile of heavy quilts and down comforters could keep David warm. So the king's attendants began a search throughout Israel for a beautiful, young virgin to care for the king as his personal nurse and to keep him warm at night.[1]

Abishag, from Shunem, was chosen on account of her youth and beauty. The king's attendants figured if anyone could warm David up, she could. It is important to note that the Bible specifically states that the relationship was not sexual (see 1 Kings 1:4). Abishag was a nurse rather than a lover, and she waited on King David as his personal caregiver. She saw that he was given the proper respect and received the attention he needed in the final season of his life. She fed him, bathed him, soothed any physical pain he had, and provided him with the warmth he could not generate himself. In short, Abishag gave comfort and eased David's last days.

About this time, Adonijah made a bid to succeed his father, David, as king. When Bathsheba went to the aged David to tell him of Adonijah's actions to claim the throne, Abishag was present, attending David. David immediately established Solomon as king, putting an end to Adonijah's play for the crown.

After the death of David, Adonijah went to Bathsheba, Solomon's mother, with a request. Knowing it would be difficult for the new king to refuse a request from his mother, Adonijah asked her to intercede with Solomon on his behalf. Adonijah acknowledged Solomon's right to the throne, then made a significant request—that he be given Abishag as his wife.

Bathsheba proceeded to make the request of Solomon. But Solomon, who had promised her in advance that her request would not be denied, was livid, not only rejecting the request, but considering it treasonous. It was clear to Solomon that Adonijah was making another bid for the throne.[2] Solomon had tolerated Adonijah's first attempt to seize the throne; he would not tolerate Adonijah's second attempt. Orders were given for Adonijah's immediate execution. The command was carried out by Benaiah.

You can be assured that the next person who considered asking Solomon for Abishag's hand thought long and hard before making the request.

What finally became of Abishag is not recorded. It is possible that Abishag became one of Solomon's wives. Some speculate that she may even be the one beloved by Solomon in the Song of Songs.[3]

Leadership Lessons

90. The tendency when one "grows old" is to "grow cold."

As leaders age, the importance of warmth becomes very significant. But bodies are not the only things that can grow cold. Emotions can grow cold, as can passion, relationships, and the soul. A warm environment, warm relationships, and warm memories are important to keep us from growing cold.

Wise leaders will monitor the intensity of their personal ardor, giving attention to the kinds of activities and attitudes that will continue to bring warmth and vibrancy to the soul as one ages. Many experienced leaders find mentoring and coaching relationships with emerging leaders help keep their own leadership fires stoked. Peer-to-peer learning is also a strategy for adding fuel to the fire.

There is no good reason to allow yourself to grow cold as you grow old.

91. Be grateful for the people who keep you "warm."

When David began to grow cold, a search was made throughout the kingdom for someone who could keep him warm. It may be that at some point in your life you will need to make a similar search for someone—a friend whose winsomeness, wit, and warmth will take the chill off the advancing years.

Some people make you colder; some make you warmer. Be grateful for those who bring warmth to your life.

92. Caregivers who are devoted to the well-being of others contribute a vital service.

Abishag's role was of such importance that she is mentioned five times in the history of the kings of Israel. As a nurse who served an aging leader in his twilight years, Abishag shared a very human and personal relationship with David, not dissimilar to one that caregivers share with their patients. Her selfless servanthood gave dignity to a fellow human being at a time of profound need in the final season of his life. The valuable service she provided is indelibly etched in biblical history. Abishag enabled David to finish well—to serve until his successor was selected and inaugurated.

It is hard to imagine a more potentially humiliating duty than Abishag's responsibility. It is also hard to imagine a more selfless example of servanthood. Abishag apparently accepted the responsibility with grace and considered her service to David as the highest privilege and duty. One does not have to look back as far as biblical history to observe such extraordinary lives of heroic charity. A brief glance around the pews of most churches will no doubt reveal many such saints.

It is also important to note that it is not only individuals who need caregivers. Organizations, like the one you perhaps lead, also need people who provide careful concern for others. Sometimes those individuals are formal caregivers, such as chaplains. Oftentimes those individuals are informal caregivers—regular employees with an extra portion of grace and concern for others. In either case, they can be a significant blessing and provide significant service to the organization.

Questions for Leadership Development

1. How will you ensure that your passion for healthy relationships and fruitful work stays kindled as you age?

2. How can you express appreciation to the caregivers who serve individuals you love and to the caregivers who provide a valuable service to the organization you lead?

3. What other leadership lessons can be derived from the story of Abishag?

The Psalm

In Psalm 71, David celebrates not being forsaken by God in old age.

Psalm 71

[1]In you, LORD, I have taken refuge;
   let me never be put to shame.
[2]In your righteousness, rescue me and deliver me;
   turn your ear to me and save me.
[3]Be my rock of refuge,
   to which I can always go;
 give the command to save me,
   for you are my rock and my fortress.
[4]Deliver me, my God, from the hand of the wicked,
   from the grasp of those who are evil and cruel.
[5]For you have been my hope, Sovereign LORD,
   my confidence since my youth.
[6]From birth I have relied on you;
   you brought me forth from my mother's womb.
   I will ever praise you.
[7]I have become a sign to many;
   you are my strong refuge.
[8]My mouth is filled with your praise,
   declaring your splendor all day long.
[9]Do not cast me away when I am old;
   do not forsake me when my strength is gone.
[10]For my enemies speak against me;
   those who wait to kill me conspire together.
[11]They say, "God has forsaken him;
   pursue him and seize him,
   for no one will rescue him."
[12]Do not be far from me, my God;
   come quickly, God, to help me.
[13]May my accusers perish in shame;
   may those who want to harm me
   be covered with scorn and disgrace.

¹⁴As for me, I will always have hope;
    I will praise you more and more.
¹⁵My mouth will tell of your righteous deeds,
    of your saving acts all day long—
    though I know not how to relate them all.
¹⁶I will come and proclaim your mighty acts, Sovereign LORD;
    I will proclaim your righteous deeds, yours alone.
¹⁷Since my youth, God, you have taught me,
    and to this day I declare your marvelous deeds.
¹⁸Even when I am old and gray,
    do not forsake me, my God,
  till I declare your power to the next generation,
    your mighty acts to all who are to come.
¹⁹Your righteousness, God, reaches to the heavens,
    you who have done great things.
    Who is like you, God?
²⁰Though you have made me see troubles,
    many and bitter,
    you will restore my life again;
  from the depths of the earth
    you will again bring me up.
²¹You will increase my honor
    and comfort me once more.
²²I will praise you with the harp
    for your faithfulness, my God;
  I will sing praise to you with the lyre,
    Holy One of Israel.
²³My lips will shout for joy
    when I sing praise to you—
    I whom you have delivered.
²⁴My tongue will tell of your righteous acts
    all day long,
  for those who wanted to harm me
    have been put to shame and confusion.

— TWENTY-FIVE —

ADONIJAH
BROTHER AGAINST BROTHER

The Background

The story of Adonijah is told in 1 Kings 1—2. He is also mentioned in 2 Samuel 3:4 and 1 Chronicles 3:2.

The Story

When David grew old, and the question of succession was in the air, Adonijah positioned himself to acquire the throne of his father, David. Adonijah, born in Hebron, was David's fourth son. His mother was Haggith. After the deaths of his older brothers, Amnon and Absalom, Adonijah assumed he was heir to the throne.[1] Like Absalom, Adonijah was handsome, lacked the shaping influence of a father's discipline, had the charisma to amass a following, and tried to anoint himself as king. Following Absalom's example, Adonijah put together an impressive parade in his own honor, with chariots and horses, and fifty men to run ahead of him.

With the support of Joab and the priest Abiathar, Adonijah arranged his own coronation party. In order to give it an air of legitimacy, sacrifices of sheep, cattle, and fattened calves were offered. Since his father, King David, had never stood in his way before, Adonijah probably thought his actions would not be contested. He invited all his brothers, with the exception of Solomon, and nearly all the royal officials. He did not invite Zadok the priest, Nathan the prophet, Benaiah the warrior, or the special guard.

Nathan took the news of Adonijah's actions to Solomon's mother, Bathsheba, and together they determined the best way to make David aware of the coup already in progress. Bathsheba reminded David that he had promised Solomon would succeed him on the throne and told David of Adonijah's plot. Nathan, with skillful diplomacy, confirmed the news that Adonijah had proclaimed himself king, concluding with, "Is this something my lord the king has done without letting his servants know?" (1 Kings 1:27).

David immediately assured Bathsheba that Solomon would be king. Zadok the priest, Nathan the prophet, and Benaiah the warrior were summoned and given instructions to take Solomon to Gihon and anoint him king over Israel. When Solomon was crowned, the people gathered at Gihon made such noise celebrating and playing pipes, that it was heard all the way to the Stone of Zoheleth where Adonijah and his friends were feasting.

The news of Solomon's coronation had a chilling effect on Adonijah's party. The guests scattered for their lives, looking for alibis, now unwilling to be associated with the pretender king.

Adonijah himself, filled with fear, headed for the best sanctuary he knew and took hold of the horns of the altar. There he was found, clinging to the horns, seeking mercy from the new king. Solomon pardoned him for his conduct on the condition that he "shows himself to be worthy" (1 Kings 1:52) and sent Adonijah home.

Solomon's mercy on the scheming Adonijah was wasted. Adonijah still had designs for the throne, as evidenced by his attempt to marry Abishag the Shunammite. Knowing the favored position Bathsheba had with Solomon, Adonijah went to her asking for a favor—that she ask Solomon to give him Abishag to be his wife.

Bathsheba may have agreed to take Adonijah's request to King Solomon because she knew what the outcome would be. In Israelite culture, the possession of the previous king's property, especially his wives, was a sign of legitimate kingship. For Adonijah to have Abishag (she was not David's wife technically, but she would have been considered his property) would establish a foothold for Adonijah to make a legitimate claim to the throne. Bathsheba would have understood the deeper agenda hidden in Adonijah's request.

When Bathsheba relayed the request, Solomon became livid, interpreting Adonijah's request as an attempt for the throne. Regarding it as an act of treason worthy of death, Solomon immediately sent Benaiah to execute Adonijah. And thus Adonijah lost not only the throne but his life as well.

Leadership Lessons

93. Great leaders know when to act quickly and decisively.

When David learned of Adonijah's plot, he instinctively realized that Solomon needed to be immediately crowned king and gave instructions that resulted in Solomon's swift coronation. David's response was wise, quick, and decisive.

There are occasions when leaders have the luxury of time. Some decisions can be considered for long periods as data is gathered and consequences are considered. Other decisions are urgent and time-sensitive, requiring immediate action. When time is of the essence, the lack of immediate action is itself a decision. Often the cost of indecisiveness is undesirable and unnecessary consequences.

Some leaders intuitively know when circumstances call for an immediate decision and urgent action. Other leaders, who may not be gifted with this intuition, will need to develop the skill of accurately discerning which decisions require immediate judgment and which decisions allow further reflection and consideration. Case studies and role-playing exercises can be valuable in this regard.

94. Advisers who can diplomatically provide needed information in a timely manner are essential for a leader's success.

What Nathan did for David was invaluable. Nathan made certain that David had the information and data needed to make a timely decision. Bathsheba similarly provided the same kind of valuable information when she brought Solomon news of Adonijah's request.

Leaders are best served when they have individuals on their team who can provide factual information in an opportune and tactful manner.

95. Children who are privileged and pampered can easily grow up to be adults who are self-absorbed and overly ambitious.

David was negligent in fulfilling his parental duties. He had exercised no control over Adonijah, never crossed him, and never pained him with discipline. Adonijah, good-looking and spoiled, had seen his siblings avoid their father's discipline when they committed rape and murder, and he reasoned that his actions would result in similar indifference. He was mistaken.

In spite of a very close call with death, Adonijah refused to put aside his aggressive ambition. By whatever means necessary, he was determined to get what he wanted. The request Adonijah made of Bathsheba revealed his desire. While his mouth said "Abishag," his heart said "throne." He still believed the kingship should have been his. Further indication of Adonijah's rebellious attitude is his statement that all Israel expected him to be king. It is easy for leaders who are excessively ambitious to overestimate their appeal. "All Israel looked to me as their king" (1 Kings 2:15) was a drastic overstatement of the facts.

Ambition is not always wrong. The world would grow lazy and stagnant without ambition. But if ambition is not ruled by righteousness, if it is not tempered by love and consideration for others, it becomes greed. Sinful ambition has led to tyranny, oppression, war, and multitudes of crimes and transgressions that have resulted in much human suffering.

Questions for Leadership Development

1. How does a leader know when to act decisively, and when to exercise patience and restraint?

2. How might Adonijah's story have been different had he been willing to embrace humility?

3. When is it appropriate for a leader to show mercy, and when is it not appropriate?

4. How can a leader know the difference between proper ambition and sinful ambition?

5. What other leadership lessons can be derived from the story of Adonijah?

The Psalm

In Psalm 37, David contrasts the fate of the wicked and the fate of the righteous. He is assured that evildoers and those who make wicked plans will ultimately come to judgment, and that the Lord will ultimately vindicate those who act righteously.

Psalm 37

Of David.

¹Do not fret because of those who are evil
    or be envious of those who do wrong;
²for like the grass they will soon wither,
    like green plants they will soon die away.
³Trust in the Lord and do good;
    dwell in the land and enjoy safe pasture.
⁴Take delight in the Lord,
    and he will give you the desires of your heart.
⁵Commit your way to the Lord;
    trust in him and he will do this:
⁶He will make your righteous reward shine like the dawn,
    your vindication like the noonday sun.
⁷Be still before the Lord
    and wait patiently for him;
 do not fret when people succeed in their ways,
    when they carry out their wicked schemes.
⁸Refrain from anger and turn from wrath;
    do not fret—it leads only to evil.
⁹For those who are evil will be destroyed,
    but those who hope in the Lord will inherit the land.
¹⁰A little while, and the wicked will be no more;
    though you look for them, they will not be found.
¹¹But the meek will inherit the land
    and enjoy peace and prosperity.
¹²The wicked plot against the righteous
    and gnash their teeth at them;

[13]but the Lord laughs at the wicked,
for he knows their day is coming.
[14]The wicked draw the sword
and bend the bow
to bring down the poor and needy,
to slay those whose ways are upright.
[15]But their swords will pierce their own hearts,
and their bows will be broken.
[16]Better the little that the righteous have
than the wealth of many wicked;
[17]for the power of the wicked will be broken,
but the LORD upholds the righteous.
[18]The blameless spend their days under the LORD's care,
and their inheritance will endure forever.
[19]In times of disaster they will not wither;
in days of famine they will enjoy plenty.
[20]But the wicked will perish:
Though the LORD's enemies are like the flowers of the field,
they will be consumed, they will go up in smoke.
[21]The wicked borrow and do not repay,
but the righteous give generously;
[22]those the LORD blesses will inherit the land,
but those he curses will be destroyed.
[23]The LORD makes firm the steps
of the one who delights in him;
[24]though he may stumble, he will not fall,
for the LORD upholds him with his hand.
[25]I was young and now I am old,
yet I have never seen the righteous forsaken
or their children begging bread.
[26]They are always generous and lend freely;
their children will be a blessing.
[27]Turn from evil and do good;
then you will dwell in the land forever.
[28]For the LORD loves the just

and will not forsake his faithful ones.
Wrongdoers will be completely destroyed;
the offspring of the wicked will perish.
29The righteous will inherit the land
and dwell in it forever.
30The mouths of the righteous utter wisdom,
and their tongues speak what is just.
31The law of their God is in their hearts;
their feet do not slip.
32The wicked lie in wait for the righteous,
intent on putting them to death;
33but the LORD will not leave them in the power of the wicked
or let them be condemned when brought to trial.
34Hope in the LORD
and keep his way.
He will exalt you to inherit the land;
when the wicked are destroyed, you will see it.
35I have seen a wicked and ruthless man
flourishing like a luxuriant native tree,
36but he soon passed away and was no more;
though I looked for him, he could not be found.
37Consider the blameless, observe the upright;
a future awaits those who seek peace.
38But all sinners will be destroyed;
there will be no future for the wicked.
39The salvation of the righteous comes from the LORD;
he is their stronghold in time of trouble.
40The LORD helps them and delivers them;
he delivers them from the wicked and saves them,
because they take refuge in him.

— TWENTY-SIX —

SOLOMON
NO SUCCESS WITHOUT A SUCCESSOR

The Background

The story of Solomon and David is told in 2 Samuel 12:24; 1 Kings 1—2; 1 Chronicles 22; 28—29. The story of Solomon following David's death is told in 1 Kings 3—11 and 2 Chronicles 1—9.

Solomon is also mentioned in 2 Samuel 5:14; 1 Kings 12; 14:21, 26; 21:7; 2 Kings 23:13; 24:13; 25:16; 1 Chronicles 3:5, 10; 6:10, 32; 14:4; 18:8; 23:1; 2 Chronicles 10—13; 30:26; 33:7; 35:3-4; Psalms 72; 127; Proverbs 1:1; 10:1; 25:1; Ecclesiastes 1:1; Song of Songs 1:1, 5; 3:7, 9, 11; 8:11, 12; Jeremiah 52:20. He is also mentioned several times in the New Testament: Matthew 1:6, 7; 6:29; 12:42; Luke 11:31; 12:27; John 10:23; Acts 3:11; 5:12; 7:47.

The Story

Solomon, whose mother was Bathsheba, was born in Jerusalem, the son of David and the third and last king of a united Israel. Little is revealed of Solomon's early life, other than that Nathan, acting on instructions from God, gave him the name Jedidiah, "beloved of the Lord," to signal God's favor. His mother "insisted on calling him Solomon, which is traditionally understood to derive from the Hebrew word for peace, *shalom*."[1]

It was the intervention of Bathsheba and Nathan, followed by the prompt action of David, that allowed Solomon to ascend to the throne when his half-brother Adonijah made a bold move for the kingship. Upon hearing of Adonijah's attempted coup, David reaffirmed the promise he had made to Bathsheba concerning their son Solomon, and promptly sent Zadok, Nathan, and Benaiah to anoint Solomon as king at Gihon. In order to leave no doubt as to his wishes, David had Solomon mounted on the king's own mule.

Meanwhile, Adonijah was hosting his friends at a party reminiscent of an election night campaign celebration when they heard the noise of an even larger celebration. They learned the cause of that festivity—that David had proclaimed Solomon king—and were all filled with fear. The guests scattered to their homes and Adonijah made a beeline for the altar to seek mercy from the new king. Solomon issued a conditional pardon and sent Adonijah home with instructions to be on his best behavior.

David did two things that significantly helped Solomon start well. First, he provided resources and plans for the construction of the temple. David had already begun to amass construction materials and make extensive preparations for the building of the temple, even though it would not be constructed during his reign. Dressed stone, marble, iron, bronze, gold, silver, and cedar logs were stockpiled for the massive project. In addition to the resources of the kingdom, David also gave of his personal possessions—gold and silver—and provided an opportunity for the people of Israel to participate in an offering for the construction of the temple. The people responded by giving gold, silver, bronze, iron, and precious stones. David also provided Solomon with blueprints for the building of the temple and detailed plans for the related infrastructure, furnishings, and work schedules.

Second, David gathered together all the officials of Israel to publicly announce the kingship of Solomon and give Solomon his blessing. In a huge public ceremony that followed Solomon's initial anointing at Gihon, David announced Solomon's appointment and decreed that the building of the temple would be Solomon's first priority. This was David's public "passing of the torch" to Solomon. David declared that Solomon and the kingdom of Israel would have peace and rest on every side during his reign. Finally, David prayed that Solomon would have success, discretion, understanding, and that he would obey the law of the Lord.[2] When David gave Solomon the charge to build the temple, he encouraged him with words similar to those the Lord used to encourage Joshua: "Be strong and courageous, and do the work. Do not be afraid or discouraged, for the LORD God, my God, is with you. He will not fail you or forsake you" (1 Chron. 28:20). David's charge included a challenge that has undoubtedly been repeated many times in similar settings: "So be strong, act like a man, and observe what the LORD your God requires" (1 Kings 2:2-3).

David's final words to his successor, no doubt spoken confidentially, contained final instructions and directives about how to handle two people David viewed as potential threats to the kingdom. The individuals named were Joab and Shimei.

Joab, after Adonijah's second failed attempt to gain the throne, knew that Solomon would be looking for him next. He sought sanctuary by running into the tent of the Lord and taking hold of the horns of the altar, but Solomon saw in this an opportunity to fulfill one of his father's last commands. Joab's days were ended there in the tent at the hand of Benaiah.

Shimei was placed under house arrest and advised that he, too, would be executed if he strayed from his home. Three years later, perhaps thinking that Solomon had forgotten his vow, Shimei traveled to Gath in search of two of his slaves who had run away. When he returned, he learned that Solomon's memory was still good. Shimei was immediately executed by Benaiah.

By the time of his death, King Solomon's legacy was secure. His crowning achievement was the building of the temple of his father's dreams, an undertaking that took seven years to complete. He then proceeded to build a palace for himself that took thirteen years to build. Solomon would become known for his wisdom, his wealth, his wives, and his writing. His wisdom, which he sought from God, is legendary. His wealth, the accumulation of an entire reign, was enormous. "The LORD highly exalted Solomon in the sight of all Israel and bestowed on him royal splendor such as no king over Israel ever had before" (1 Chron. 29:25). Solomon's many marriages—he had seven hundred wives and three hundred concubines—were designed to strengthen his kingdom politically through alliances but also weakened him spiritually. Ecclesiastes, Proverbs, and the Song of Songs have all been attributed to Solomon. The Bible portrays Solomon as great in wisdom, wealth, and power, but ultimately as a king whose sin, including idolatry, resulted in the kingdom being torn in two during the reign of his son Rehoboam.

Leadership Lessons

96. There is no success without a successor.

If the welfare of the organization is important to a departing leader, the effective transfer of responsibility to the next leader will be an important concern.[3] At the time of David's last days, Israel had not dealt with the issue of the transfer of power. The question of who was to succeed David was an open one.

David, unlike most leaders, had the privilege of naming his own successor. While most leaders often do not have the opportunity to name their successor, they can help ensure the success of their successor. For a successor to start well, the predecessor must end well and provide for a healthy transition. This is an important component of "finishing strong."

I serve in a denomination that, like most denominations, does not grant to pastors the privilege of naming their successors. Pastors do, however, have the opportunity to prepare the churches they serve for succession. They can accomplish that by taking the same action David took in preparing Israel for succession. First, David did his best to ensure his successor had the resources adequate to accomplish the top priority. Leaders whose season of service to an organization is coming to a close are sometimes tempted to drain off resources for their own benefit. David refused to do this.

Second, David prepared the nation for a successful transition in leadership by publicly blessing his successor, speaking well of him, and assuring the nation that the future looked bright. The blessing of a predecessor costs little but is worth much. That action alone can help ensure the success of the next leader by inspiring confidence. Speaking highly of the one who will follow you will help prepare the organization to look to the future with hope and anticipation. Providing adequate resources for a successor to begin well, and public affirmation for them to begin strong, are the two most significant gifts leaders can provide their successors.

Some leaders do far better at succession planning than others. David obviously did better at succession planning than did Solomon. Moses did a better job of succession planning than did Joshua. This may be one reason why both David and Moses are held in higher esteem than either Solomon or Joshua. There is no lasting success without a successful succession. Perhaps the most important thing any leader does to help ensure the continued health and vitality of the organization is to prepare the way for a successful succession.

Albert Mohler observes, "Leaders are made by other leaders, and are made better by other leaders, and go on to make yet more leaders."[4] Perhaps the most important thing that great leaders do is "to make yet more leaders."

97. A predecessor's "unfinished business" often becomes a new leader's "first order of business."[5]

Leaders can provide their successors valuable information that will help ensure a healthy transition and set up successors for success. In his final days, David publicly gave instructions and encouragement to Solomon. It certainly seemed to help. Solomon, with God's blessing, lost no time in beginning construction on the temple and in continuing to make Israel a strong and prosperous nation.

David also provided Solomon with confidential instructions about some delicate matters, and directives about how to handle two people whom David judged to be potential threats to the kingdom. While David instructed Solomon to show kindness to Barzillai, he also counseled Solomon to deal decisively with Joab and Shimei. For whatever reason, David did not deal with them himself, but left them to Solomon. Essentially, David was saying, "As you're getting started, Solomon, you're going to have to take care of some unfinished business."

David's unfinished business was that he had not effectively dealt with two people who had a propensity to undermine the integrity of the kingdom. David knew that Solomon would have to take decisive action to deal with them. The significant risks they posed to the kingdom needed to be eliminated, and it became Solomon's responsibility to deal with those individuals.

Whether it is a kingdom, a business, a church, or a team, none of us can afford to surround ourselves with people that will undermine the integrity of the organization we lead or the effectiveness of the mission we have been given. Such individuals will need to be attended to with wisdom, fairness, and decisiveness.

98. Leadership is a learned art, and many of the lessons are free.

Undoubtedly, there were several factors that contributed to Solomon's rise to leadership of Israel. He had both nature and nurture on his side. Genetics definitely played a role. Solomon's father was a great leader, and his mother was not only beautiful but politically astute herself. Being raised in the palace of the king would have offered Solomon a front-row seat in the real-life classroom of the leadership of a nation.

Not many aspiring leaders will have the advantages Solomon enjoyed. But for anyone who wishes to learn the art of leadership, many of the lessons are free to those who would take advantage of them (the lessons have already been paid for by those who took the risks or suffered the failures). In addition to the plethora of books, magazines, articles, and blogs on leadership, all one has to do is study the successes and failure of the many leaders each of us encounter daily.

99. Leaders leave a legacy.

David served as king for forty years. His long tenure allowed him the opportunity to make an enduring difference. But David was not king forever. His leadership ended as did his life.

There comes a day in the life of every leader when the work is done, due to resignation, replacement, retirement, or death. The term of leadership always expires. Inevitably, someone will take over for each of us. Ours is "a temporary stewardship."[6] But those who prove themselves to be good stewards of their organization's mission, vision, values, and resources have the opportunity to leave a legacy that will continue to guide and support their organization for years after their departure.

May you and I be such leaders.

Questions for Leadership Development

1. What blessings have you inherited from your predecessor?

2. What are you doing now to help ensure your successor's success?

3. How would you feel if someone else, rather than you, has the opportunity to see your dream become reality?

4. What "unfinished business" should you deal with before succession takes place?

5. What will it look like for you to "finish strong" in your present assignment?

6. What other leadership lessons can be derived from the story of Solomon?

The Psalm

Psalm 72 contains David's prayer for the success of his son Solomon and is a model of how to accomplish a healthy leadership transition.

Psalm 72

Of Solomon.

¹Endow the king with your justice, O God,
    the royal son with your righteousness.
²May he judge your people in righteousness,
    your afflicted ones with justice.
³May the mountains bring prosperity to the people,
    the hills the fruit of righteousness.
⁴May he defend the afflicted among the people
    and save the children of the needy;
    may he crush the oppressor.
⁵May he endure as long as the sun,
    as long as the moon, through all generations.
⁶May he be like rain falling on a mown field,
    like showers watering the earth.
⁷In his days may the righteous flourish
    and prosperity abound till the moon is no more.
⁸May he rule from sea to sea
    and from the River to the ends of the earth.
⁹May the desert tribes bow before him
    and his enemies lick the dust.
¹⁰May the kings of Tarshish and of distant shores
    bring tribute to him.
  May the kings of Sheba and Seba
    present him gifts.
¹¹May all kings bow down to him
    and all nations serve him.
¹²For he will deliver the needy who cry out,
    the afflicted who have no one to help.

[13]He will take pity on the weak and the needy
   and save the needy from death.
[14]He will rescue them from oppression and violence,
   for precious is their blood in his sight.
[15]Long may he live!
   May gold from Sheba be given him.
 May people ever pray for him
   and bless him all day long.
[16]May grain abound throughout the land;
   on the tops of the hills may it sway.
 May the crops flourish like Lebanon
   and thrive like the grass of the field.
[17]May his name endure forever;
   may it continue as long as the sun.
 Then all nations will be blessed through him,
   and they will call him blessed.
[18]Praise be to the LORD God, the God of Israel,
   who alone does marvelous deeds.
[19]Praise be to his glorious name forever;
   may the whole earth be filled with his glory.
 Amen and Amen.
[20]This concludes the prayers of David son of Jesse.

EPILOGUE
JESUS, SON OF DAVID

The Background

The relationship between Jesus and David is referred to in Matthew 1:1; 9:27; 12:23; 15:22; 20:30-31; 21:9, 15; 22:42; Mark 10:47-48; 12:35; Luke 1:32; 3:31; 18:38-39; 20:41; John 7:42; Acts 13:22-36; Romans 1:3; 2 Timothy 2:8; Revelation 5:5.

The Story

A thousand years after the reign of King David, the understanding that the Messiah would be a descendant of David had broad acceptance. As Kirsch notes, "Judaism and Christianity, which contend with each other on so many other issues, share the same thrilling idea that David's blood will flow in the veins of the Messiah."[1] During the time of Jesus' ministry, the Jewish community anticipated that the "Son of David" would deliver Israel and usher in a new kingdom.

Several Old Testament passages seem to allude to this idea, using that title to foreshadow the life and ministry of Jesus. Isaiah 9:6-7 indicates that the Messiah is to sit on the throne of David:

> For to us a child is born, to us a son is given, and the government will be on his shoulders. And he will be called Wonderful Counselor, Mighty God, Everlasting Father, Prince of Peace. Of the greatness of his government and peace there will be no end. He will reign on David's throne and over his

kingdom, establishing and upholding it with justice and righteousness from that time on and forever. The zeal of the LORD Almighty will accomplish this.

Psalm 132:11 specifies the necessity of the Messiah being born in the direct line of David: "The LORD swore an oath to David, a sure oath he will not revoke: 'One of your own descendants I will place on your throne.'" In 2 Samuel 7:16 God promised David, "Your house and your kingdom will endure forever before me; your throne will be established forever."

The New Testament then opens with Matthew's introduction of a new King. He argues that Jesus is the Messiah, "the son of David, the son of Abraham" (Matt. 1:1), in part, by effectively linking Jesus to both the father of Israel, Abraham, and to Israel's greatest king, David. Matthew proceeds to give the King's credentials by offering genealogical proof that Jesus is a direct descendant of both David and Abraham through Joseph, Mary's husband and Jesus' legal father.[2] Twenty-eight generations separate Jesus from David.[3]

In the first chapter of the Gospel of Luke, the angel tells Mary that God will give Jesus "the throne of his father David" (Luke 1:32). The genealogy Luke offers traces back Jesus' lineage through David and Abraham to Adam.[4] Some suggest that Luke gives Jesus' genealogy through his mother, Mary.[5] Thus, both sides of the family of Jesus are seen to have descended from David.

In the Gospels, Jesus is addressed as "Son of David" several times by people who, by faith, are seeking mercy or healing. In Matthew 9:27, two blind men refer to Jesus as "Son of David" when crying to him for mercy. Jesus restores their sight. A Canaanite woman who seeks healing and deliverance for her demon-possessed daughter,[6] the two blind men located outside Jericho who seek mercy from Jesus,[7] and blind Bartimaeus[8] all cry out to Jesus the "Son of David" for help, and receive it. The title of honor they gave Jesus acknowledged their faith in him and was understood as professing him to be the Messiah.

There are others who link Jesus with David. When Jesus heals a demon-possessed man, restoring both his sight and his voice, the people wonder aloud if Jesus might be "the Son of David" (Matt. 12:23). When Jesus rides into Jerusalem on a donkey on Palm Sunday, Matthew has the crowds shouting, "Hosanna to the Son of David!" (21:9), as do the children in the temple courts.[9] In Matthew 22:42 the crowd claims that the Messiah will be "the Son of David."

Even beyond the Gospels, the New Testament stresses the fact that Jesus is the Son of David. Peter addresses the connection in his sermon on the day of Pentecost,[10] Paul twice affirms that Jesus is a descendant of David.[11] John the Revelator hears the risen Christ say, "I am the Root and the Offspring of David" (Rev. 22:16). In all, seventeen verses in the New Testament describe Jesus as the "Son of David."

The fact that Jesus was so often referred to by this title highlights the belief of the Gospel writers that Jesus was the fulfillment of prophecy and that Jesus was literally descended from David's family line. They were identifying Jesus as the Christ, the Messiah who was promised to come.

By contrast, the religious leaders of the time were furious at the idea of Jesus being called the Son of David. They were so blinded by their own pride and prejudice they could not see what sightless beggars could see—that Jesus was the Messiah they had been waiting for all their lives. They hated Jesus because he would not give them the prestige they thought they deserved, so when they heard the people hailing Jesus as the Savior, they became enraged and plotted to kill him.[12]

Jesus, knowing their thoughts, further confounded the scribes and Pharisees by asking them to explain the meaning of the "Son of David" title.[13] He was making the point that "Son of David" was more than a physical reference—it described the One who would come as Messiah and was deserving of worship. The teachers of the Law either would not or could not answer the question, and their ineffectiveness as teachers was exposed.

Leadership Lesson

100. Whom you follow is even more important than who follows you.

The New Testament opens with Matthew making a case for following Jesus. He does this in several ways, most notably by providing evidence that Jesus is of the line of David. The prophets foretold that this would be true of the Messiah. While not the only proof that Jesus is the Messiah, the tracing of Jesus' lineage directly to David shows that Jesus met this important qualification. Through Jesus' genealogy, Matthew begins building the case that Jesus, Son of David, is worthy of being followed.

Whom you follow is important. This is true in terms of succession. It is especially true in terms of leadership influence. Whom you follow, emulate, and allow to influence you is of utmost importance.

Following Jesus certainly has implications far beyond developing one's leadership potential. The primary reason to follow Jesus is not to improve one's leadership skills, but because salvation is found in no other name (Acts 4:12). More than just emulating him, or being influenced by his life and ministry, Jesus is worthy of being followed because he is Savior and risen Lord.

While many in the pages of the New Testament followed Jesus, there were also many who did not. Those who did follow Jesus—his disciples—became significant leaders themselves, their hearts and characters transformed by his grace.

May we learn what they learned—that Jesus, the Son of David, is worthy of being followed.

Questions for Leadership Development

1. Whom are you following?

2. Who is following you?

3. What other leadership lessons can be derived from the relationship between David and Jesus?

The Psalm

Psalm 110 is one of the messianic psalms, which Christians believe point in anticipation to Jesus.[14] Christians interpret Psalm 110 as David celebrating the future coming of Jesus. As this psalm was also quoted by Jesus,[15] it appears that Jesus was reaching back to David in much the same way as David was reaching forward to Jesus.

Psalm 110

Of David. A psalm.

[1]The LORD says to my lord:
  "Sit at my right hand
    until I make your enemies
    a footstool for your feet."
[2]The LORD will extend your mighty scepter from Zion, saying,
    "Rule in the midst of your enemies!"
[3]Your troops will be willing
    on your day of battle.
  Arrayed in holy splendor,
    your young men will come to you
    like dew from the morning's womb.
[4]The LORD has sworn
    and will not change his mind:
  "You are a priest forever,
    in the order of Melchizedek."
[5]The Lord is at your right hand;
    he will crush kings on the day of his wrath.
[6]He will judge the nations, heaping up the dead
    and crushing the rulers of the whole earth.
[7]He will drink from a brook along the way,
    and so he will lift his head high.

INDEX
100 LESSONS FOR LEADERS

1. God knows where to find you.
2. Emerging leaders need experienced leaders to bless them.
3. The leaders of the next generation might not resemble the leaders of this generation.
4. Recognizing potential—and helping to bring it out—is one of the most critical roles of leadership.
5. Retirement need not be the end of a leader's contributions.
6. Your lasting legacy may be your children.
7. The one who best knows your past may least know your future.
8. Leaders make people nervous.
9. Leadership is a matter of the heart.
10. Nothing reveals your heart like your response to the promotions of others.
11. Leadership is not spectatorship.
12. Leaders are not derailed by criticism.
13. Effective leadership and servanthood are inseparable.
14. Leaders prove their capacity to be faithful in the big challenges by being faithful in the little challenges.
15. Learn to face challenges with the unique weapons and armor with which God has gifted you.
16. The enemy wants to take you out.
17. Leaders face challenges with courage and confidence in God.
18. Important relationships require time, commitment, and cultivation if they are to be strong and healthy.
19. Bitterness can result in barrenness.
20. A covenant friendship is a special kind of relationship.
21. A covenant friendship is marked by a kindredness of spirit.
22. A covenant friendship is marked by loyalty.

23. A covenant friendship is marked by encouragement.
24. A covenant friendship is marked by unselfishness.
25. A covenant friendship can bless succeeding generations.
26. Every leader needs a covenant friendship.
27. Your presence in a place of worship does not guarantee that you are a person of worship.
28. Someone is always looking.
29. When leaders deceive—even for good reasons—the negative consequences can prove devastating.
30. If you have to pretend to be someone or something you are not, perhaps you are not in the right place.
31. For good and for ill, decisions you make affect the lives of others.
32. Our good fortune sometimes has everything to do with God's graceful providence.
33. It is easy for leaders to overreact to slights, especially when under stress.
34. The "art of de-escalation" is a valuable skill in defusing a volatile situation.
35. Acknowledge, with gratitude and grace, the debt you owe another.
36. Hurt feelings never justify hurtful actions.
37. Good leaders have the wisdom to change their course when it becomes apparent they are going in the wrong direction.
38. Most leaders will have a few followers who want to go too far in their zeal.
39. It is not enough for leaders to be strong and effective; leaders must also have self-control and wisdom.
40. Leaders must be able to determine what risks are acceptable.
41. Jealousy will destroy your effectiveness as a leader.
42. In leadership, how you finish is more important than how you start.

43. You do not have to be the first one to throw the spear to be a spear thrower.

44. It is foolish to not eliminate Amalekites.

45. Speak well of your predecessor.

46. Leaders usually either become better or they become bitter.

47. Leaders attract followers like themselves.

48. The hardships faced by leaders are usually matched, and often exceeded, by the hardships faced by their families.

49. On the worst day of your life, it makes sense to turn to God.

50. When the Lord blesses you, consider blessing others.

51. It is possible for opponents to become allies.

52. Honorable leaders will not condone the dishonorable actions of their followers.

53. Sometimes the real leader is not the one with the title.

54. He who makes the decisions is king.

55. Heredity is no guarantee that one will be a good leader.

56. Patient waiting, rather than rash action, can position leaders for opportunity.

57. Be careful what you bless.

58. The means are as important as the ends.

59. As leaders build their teams, they are wise to consider character to be more essential than competency.

60. Those who grow fond of power and position will be tempted to use unjust means to maintain power and position.

61. It is better to do nothing than to take action that will compromise your own integrity.

62. Wise leaders will seek wisdom and direction from God.

63. Not everyone who served your predecessor well will necessarily serve you well.

64. Leaders need to know the most appropriate ways to deal with individuals who would undermine their leadership.

65. Each of us is in need of grace.

66. Each of us is offered grace.
67. Each of us can extend grace.
68. Leaders keep their promises and are careful what they promise.
69. Leaders must, at all costs, avoid an entitlement mentality.
70. Vision can be both a blessing and a curse.
71. Leaders must avoid viewing individuals as objects to be used for their own benefits.
72. Isolation is the breeding ground for temptation.
73. There is a fatal progression with sin.
74. Reality cannot be ignored.
75. God's grace is greater than a leader's sin.
76. The contrast between loyalty and disloyalty—between faithfulness and unfaithfulness—is stark.
77. Bad decisions breed bad decisions.
78. Sooner or later, a leader's sin is always found out.
79. When sin is found out, there will be complications and consequences.
80. The sin of one leader can result in the suffering of many other people.
81. It may be that your vision will be accomplished by your successor, not you.
82. Every leader needs someone to speak truth into his or her life.
83. While forgiveness will remove the guilt of sin, the consequences of sin almost always remain.
84. Leadership begins at home.
85. Unbridled ambition is disaster in the making.
86. Nothing reveals a leader's heart like the response to betrayal.
87. Decisiveness and the ability to appropriately allocate available resources can be key to survival.
88. Assets can become liabilities.
89. Leaders who erect monuments in honor of themselves seldom have monuments in their honor erected by others.

90. The tendency when one "grows old" is to "grow cold."

91. Be grateful for the people who keep you "warm."

92. Caregivers who are devoted to the well-being of others contribute a vital service.

93. Great leaders know when to act quickly and decisively.

94. Advisers who can diplomatically provide needed information in a timely manner are essential for a leader's success.

95. Children who are privileged and pampered can easily grow up to be adults who are self-absorbed and overly ambitious.

96. There is no success without a successor.

97. A predecessor's "unfinished business" often becomes a new leader's "first order of business."

98. Leadership is a learned art, and many of the lessons are free.

99. Leaders leave a legacy.

100. Whom you follow is even more important than who follows you.

NOTES

Chapter 1: Samuel

1. Adapted from Frederick Buechner, *Peculiar Treasures: A Biblical Who's Who* (New York: HarperCollins, 1979), 170.

2. E. B. Long and Ulysses S. Grant, *Personal Memoirs of Ulysses S. Grant* (Cambridge, MA: Da Capo Press, 2001), 359.

3. I am indebted to David Wilson for this saying.

4. A. W. Tozer, *Warfare of the Spirit: Religious Rituals versus the Presence of the Indwelling Christ* (Camp Hill, PA: WingSpread Publishers, 2006), 174.

5. Albert Mohler, *The Conviction to Lead: 25 Principles for Leadership that Matters* (Bloomington, MN: Bethany House Publishers, 2012), 211-12.

6. It is interesting to note that retired United States military officers may be recalled by the president until death. One wonders what impact it might have if the church took sufficient advantage of the same prerogative in recalling her retired leaders.

Chapter 2: Jesse

1. William H. Willimon, *The Last Word: Insights about the Church and Ministry* (Nashville: Abingdon Press, 2000), 108-9.

2. I am indebted to Joe McLamb for this insight.

Chapter 3: Eliab

1. Eliab is called Elihu in 1 Chronicles 27:18.

2. See 1 Samuel 17:28.

3. See Acts 13:22.

4. See 1 Corinthians 12:26.

Chapter 4: Goliath

1. Buechner, *Peculiar Treasures*, 47.

2. See 1 Samuel 17:55.

3. Charles R. Swindoll, *David: A Man of Passion and Destiny* (Nashville: Thomas Nelson, 2000), 38.

4. Ibid., 20.

5. Ibid.

6. See 1 Peter 5:8.

Chapter 5: Michal

1. See 2 Samuel 21:8 and footnote in the NIV.

2. Steven McKenzie suggests that David prevented Michal from having children in order to extinguish the line of Saul and deny potential rivals to the throne (*King David: A Biography* [New York: Oxford University Press, 2000], 137-38).

3. See 2 Samuel 21:1-9.

4. I am indebted to Joe McLamb for raising this significant question.

Chapter 6: Jonathan

1. See 2 Samuel 1.

2. See 1 Samuel 18:3-4.

3. See 1 Samuel 20:14-17, 42.

Chapter 7: Doeg

1. See 1 Samuel 14:47.

2. See Acts 13:22.

3. Jim Elliff, "Doeg the Edomite: A Man after Saul's Own Heart," *bulletininserts.org*, http://www.bulletininserts.org/bulletininsert.aspx?bulletininsert_id=384, accessed May 13, 2014.

Chapter 8: Achish

1. Swindoll, *David*, 184.

2. Ibid., 192.

3. Ibid., 184.

4. See Joan Comay and Ronald Browning, *Who's Who in the Bible* (New York: Bonanza Books, 1980), 36. Achish is also called Abimelek in Psalm 34.

Chapter 9: Abigail

1. See 1 Samuel 25:22.

Chapter 10: Nabal

1. John Trapp, *John Trapp Complete Commentary*, 1 Samuel 25:39, *studylight.org*, http://www.studylight.org/com/jtc/view.cgi?bk=1sa&ch=25#1, accessed May 13, 2014.

2. See Psalms 27:14; 33:20; 37:7; 38:15; 40:1; 119:166; 130:5-6.

3. I am indebted to Joe McLamb for this insight.

4. Holeman and Martyn introduce this memorable question: Does your leadership style tend to be more "jerk-like" or more "Christ-like"? Virginia T. Holeman and Stephen L. Martyn, *Inside the Leader's Head: Unraveling Personal Obstacles to Ministry* (Nashville: Abingdon Press, 2008).

Chapter 12: Saul

1. Robert Pinsky, *The Life of David* (New York: Random House, 2005), 25.

2. See 1 Samuel 10:20-23.

3. Pinsky, *Life of David*, 26.

4. Psalm 59, in which David prays for deliverance from his enemies, contains imagery reminiscent of this incident.

5. Pinsky, *Life of David*, 31.

6. Saul had earlier been given specific instructions from Samuel, on behalf of God, to totally destroy the Amalekites. See 1 Samuel 15:3.

7. See 2 Samuel 1:17-27.

8. For an insightful look at the character of Saul, David, and Absalom, see Gene Edwards, *A Tale of Three Kings: A Study in Brokenness* (Carol Stream, IL: Tyndale House Publishers, 1992).

9. Buechner, *Peculiar Treasures*, 173.

10. See 1 Samuel 26:21.

11. See 2 Samuel 1:17-27.

Chapter 13: Ahinoam

1. King Saul's wife was also named Ahinoam, the daughter of Ahimaaz (see 1 Sam. 14:50). Some scholars suggest that the wife of Saul and the wife of David may be, in fact, one person and that David took Ahinoam from Saul. This speculation finds support in 2 Samuel 12:8, where God tells David through the prophet Nathan, "I gave your master's house to you, and your master's wives into your arms." However, while Saul's wife is consistently identified as "daughter of Ahimaaz," David's wife is consistently identified as "of Jezreel"—an apparent differentiation of the two. With Jonathan about the same age as, if not older than, David, Ahinoam, the wife of Saul, would be too old to give birth to David's firstborn son, Amnon. It is also hard to imagine Jonathan and David being such good friends if Jonathan's mother was David's wife.

2. See 1 Samuel 30:22-25.

Chapter 14: Abner

1. Pinsky, *Life of David*, 73.

Chapter 15: Ish-Bosheth

1. Kevin J. Mellish, *1 & 2 Samuel: A Commentary in the Wesleyan Tradition, New Beacon Bible Commentary* (Kansas City: Beacon Hill Press of Kansas City, 2012), 195.

Chapter 16: Baanah and Rekab

1. NIV spelling. Also "Rechab" in most versions.

Chapter 17: Joab

1. Pinsky observes that both generals—Joab and Abner—appear at the critical points in David's career, Abner at the beginning and Joab at the end. "They serve as dual sentinels at David's entry and departure" (*Life of David*, 117).

2. Rabbah is today known as Amman, Jordan.

3. Joab may have disagreed with the census on the basis that if Israel knew the exact details of their troop strength, it would become easier for their enemies to know their true force strength.

4. Graham presents an engaging portrayal of Benaiah and David's mighty men in the *Lion of War Series*. See Cliff Graham, *Day of War* (Grand Rapids: Zondervan, 2011), and Cliff Graham, *Covenant of War* (Grand Rapids: Zondervan, 2012).

5. Mohler, *Conviction to Lead*, 107.

Chapter 18: Abiathar

1. There is some confusion created by 1 Chronicles 18:16; 24:3, 6, 31; and 2 Samuel 8:17. Some believe these passages accidentally transpose the names of Ahimelek and Abiathar. Others suggest that in addition to Abiathar's father's name being Ahimelek, Abiathar had a son named Ahimelek.

2. See 1 Samuel 3:13.

Chapter 19: Mephibosheth

1. Years later, David again spared Mephibosheth when the Gibeonites requested that seven of Saul's male descendants be given them to avenge Saul's attempted annihilation of their tribe. See 2 Samuel 21.

2. Mellish, *1 & 2 Samuel*, 222.

Chapter 20: Bathsheba

1. "Ammiel" in 1 Chronicles 3:5.

2. Dean C. Ludwig and Clinton O. Longenecker, "The Bathsheba Syndrome: The Ethical Failure of Successful Leaders," *Journal of Business Ethics* 12 (1993): 265-73.

Professors Ludwig and Longenecker of the University of Toledo's Department of Management use the story of David and Bathsheba to look at four by-products of success: loss of strategic focus, privileged access, control of resources, and inflated belief in the ability to manipulate outcomes. The authors call for ethical training programs that would prepare leaders for the trials and dilemmas associated with success. See http://ksuweb. kennesaw.edu/~uzimmerm/Notes/Ludwig+Longenecker,%20The%20 Bathsheba%20Syndrome.pdf.

3. See Acts 13:22.

4. See 1 Kings 15:5.

5. Mellish, *1 & 2 Samuel*, 228.

6. See Psalm 32:3. "When I kept silent" speaks of the danger of silence in the matter of temptation.

7. Jonathan Kirsch, *King David: The Real Life of the Man Who Ruled Israel* (New York: Ballantine Books, 2000), 186.

8. See 2 Samuel 12:25.

Chapter 21: Uriah

1. Pinsky, *Life of David*, 104.

2. I am indebted to Steve Estep for this expression.

3. Pinsky, *Life of David*, 105.

4. Mellish, *1 & 2 Samuel*, 227.

5. I am indebted to Joe McLamb for this wisdom.

Chapter 22: Nathan

1. Nathan the prophet may or may not have been the father of one of David's top soldiers (Igal) and/or a brother of a later captain in David's forces (Joel) and/or the father of two of Solomon's chieftains (Azariah and Zabud). It may be that Azariah and Zabud were the children of a son of David also named Nathan.

2. Swindoll, *David*, 268.

3. Kirsch, *King David*, 196.

Chapter 23: Absalom

1. See variant readings of 2 Samuel 15:7.

2. Buechner, *Peculiar Treasures,* 6.

3. Pinsky, *Life of David*, 134.

4. For an insightful look at the characters of Saul, David, and Absalom, see Edwards, *A Tale of Three Kings*.

5. See Acts 13:22.

6. Mohler, *Conviction to Lead*, 142.

Chapter 24: Abishag

1. The author's wife suggests that if a similar situation were to occur in our day, the purchase of an electric blanket would be more appropriate!

2. In the story of Absalom's rebellion it is noted that having sexual relations with a member of the king's household is a way of proclaiming oneself to be the new king.

3. See Song of Songs 1:5; 6:13.

Chapter 25: Adonijah

1. It appears that Kileab—David's third son—died young or was somehow unavailable or unfit to be king since no further mention is made of him.

Chapter 26: Solomon

1. Kirsch, *King David*, 200.

2. See 1 Chronicles 22:11-13.

3. See John C. Maxwell, *The 21 Irrefutable Laws of Leadership: Follow Them and People Will Follow You* (Nashville: Thomas Nelson Publishers, 1998), 215-24. Maxwell calls this "The Law of Legacy" and suggests that a leader's lasting value is measured by succession.

4. Mohler, *Conviction to Lead*, 14.

5. I owe this insight to my brother, Steve Estep.

6. Mohler, *Conviction to Lead*, 200.

Epilogue

1. Kirsch, *King David*, 5.

2. In Matthew 1:20, Joseph, husband of Mary, is also called "son of David" by the angel.

3. See Matthew 1:17.

4. See Luke 3:23-38.

5. Charles L. Childers, *Beacon Bible Commentary, Vol. VI, "Luke"* (Kansas City: Beacon Hill Press, 1964), 38.

6. See Matthew 15:22.

7. See Matthew 20:30.

8. See Mark 10:46-47; Luke 18:38.

9. See Matthew 21:15.

10. See Acts 2:29-36.

11. See Romans 1:3; 2 Timothy 2:8.

12. See Matthew 21:15; Luke 19:47.

13. See Mark 12:35-37.

14. See also Psalms 2; 22; 89:3-4; 132:11.

15. See Mark 12:35-37.